ENGLISH RECUSANT LITERATURE
1558–1640

Selected and Edited by
D. M. ROGERS

Volume 133

Private Instructions
1634

ANTHONY BATT
A Poore Mans Mite
1639

ANTONIO POSSEVINO
A Treatise
of . . . the Masse
1570

Private Instructions
1634

The Scolar Press
1973

ISBN o 85417 934 8

*Published and Printed in Great Britain by
The Scolar Press Limited, 20 Main Street,
Menston, Yorkshire, England*

NOTE

The following works are reproduced (original size) with permission:

1) *Private instructions*, 1634, (anon.), from a copy in Trinity College Library, Dublin, by permission of the Board of Trinity College.

Not in Allison and Rogers; not in STC.

2) Anthony Batt, *A poore mans mite*, 1639, from a copy in the library of St. Mary's Abbey, Colwich, by permission of the Lady Abbess.

Reference: Allison and Rogers 74; not in STC.

3) Antonio Possevino, *A treatise of . . . the Masse*, 1570, from a copy in the library of St. Mary's Seminary, Oscott, by permission of the President.

Reference: Allison and Rogers 659; not in STC.

PRIVATE
INSTRVCTIONS
LATELY SENT

From a Cath. Gentleman beyond the
Sea's, vnto his Proteſtant Friend
in I R E L A N D, for his Search into
matters of Religion.

*With Certaine Reaſons, why the Truth
being once found out, all further
Conference is needleſſe.*

Quærite, & inuenietis. Luc. 11.

Seeke, and you shall find.

Anno Domini M. D C. XXXIIII.

TO THE READER.

GOOD READER.

A Gentleman of the Irish Nation by birth, but throgh the iniury of the tymes, by profeſsion a Proteſtant, hauing occaſion to make a iourney lately into the Low-Countryes, and there ſeing the vniforme Exerciſe of the Cath. Religion to be practiſed in euery place, began to wonder; and by a further Inquiry, vnderſtanding that in all *France*, *Spaine*, *Italy*, *Polony*, and the moſt parts of *Germany* by far, the very ſame, without any alteration, was publikely exerciſed, & none other; fell into a further admiration, and ſeriouſly to ponder in his thoughts, the weight of ſo great a matter. Wherupon finding in himſelfe, no great obſtacle why he ſhould not alſo imbrace the ſame generall Religion, which the knew to be likewiſe ordinarily exerciſed, though in a priuate man-

A 2   ner,

ner, in his owne Countrey of *Ireland* ; he
presently wrote a Letter vnto a Kinsman
of his residing in *Spayne*, a Gentleman of
quality, and good vnderstanding, impar-
ting vnto him his whole mynd and incli-
nation, and withall requesting his aduise
in so important a busines, by informing
him how, and by what meanes he might
best accomplish this his desire, conside-
ring he had byn, for the most part of his
yeares, brought vp in the Court of England, & in the Religion there publickly
professed. At the receyt of this letter,
his said friend sent vnto him these Instructions, or Aduertisements following: the
which, although penned, and directed to
a priuate and particuler person ; yet because they may be profitable both to thy
selfe (GOOD READER) and others
that may chance to fall into the same per-
plexity, I haue thought good to make
publike.

ADVER-

ADVERTISMENTS
FOR YOVR SEARCH
INTO RELIGION.

T BEING without faith impoſſible to pleaſe God, (*Heb. 11.*) and as God is but one, ſo true faith being but one (*Epheſ: 4 :*) I wiſh you to embrace that graue counſayl of S. Paul to the Corinthians: *Corin. ep: 2. cap. 13. v. 5.* to whom he ſaith: *Trie your ſelues, vvheather yee are in the faith: examine your ſelues.* And S. Paul in the wordes that there follow, proſequuteth this point ſo, as if that careleſnes in triall of faith, were a token that the careleſſe is a reprobate, which token I ſee not in you, becauſe you ſhew your ſelfe carefull to ſearch into the truth, and becauſe you make this triall by a kinde of reading (which for

this

this prefent I wil not condemne)ther-
fore I fend you thefe cõfiderations of
fome vndoubted truthes, to which
you ought to haue an eye in your
fearch and reading.

1 The firft vncontrouerted and certaine truth is, that faith is a firme and
affured affent of the foule, by which,
wee doe beleeue doctrines wherof
we fee no euident reafon, and therfore not to be beleeued but for fome
moft fubftantial authoritie; wherfore
I muft haue an eie in what religion
are more meanes of certainty & affu-
rance, and a more eftablifhed authoritie: which when I haue feene I may
embrace that more reafonablie and
chriftianlie then the other.

The Proteftant will be found to
refufe in deede (though in word, he
pretendeth fome other grounds) all
other grounds befides a fpirit which
perfwadeth him to this or that point

of

of faith : which spirite wheather it be of God or of the Diuel, or of his owne discourse he is not assured, nor hath any meanes to try. For the first thing that he hath is the spirite, by which he afterwards persuadeth him selfe, that these and these writings be Gods scriptures. Then by the same he defineth, that in these sillables, this and this was Gods meaning, as if he should say, I am fully assured this doctrine is true, because I think it is true and consequentlie, that very truth which he drew from the catholique church, and is content to retaine, (as the acknowledging of the blessed Trinitie, or the Incarnation) he holdeth not by Christian faith, but by selfe opinion in vncertaintie.

The Catholique will be found to confesse, that his owne spirite is insufficient of it selfe, to instruct him what to beleeue of God, or how to

A 3

serue him, and that though him selfe,
haue great witte, industry, learning,
and vse to reade scriptures: yet that
without some sufficient exteriour te-
ftimony of truth, it is daungerous to
geue credit to euery motion of his
inward perswasiō, be it neuer so probable. And therfore that he relyeth
vpon Christ (whom the most prudent
man in the world, ought vpon most
reasonable motiues to beleeue to be
God) who as he praied for, and with
his owne blood priced, and paied for
a church: So he prouided her the perpetuall assistáce of the spirit of Truth,
which in Pentecost he powred vpon
her, still to remaine with her. And
therfore chardgeth al mankinde ab-
solutelie to obey her, which (if the
true church were inuisible) no man
could doe, or if it could teach errour,
no man absolutely might in conscience doe; wherfore the catholiques
doe

doe trie al their owne cōceits of God and his seruice, by the spirit of Christ assisting the visible church, which S. Paul worthilie calleth the pillar and ground of truth; *1.Tim.3.v.15.*

2 The second vndoubted truth is. That as the true God is but one, so the true faith is but one, & giuen to bring men to vnity of iudgment, and vniformitie of proceeding, that al faithful people may be at vnitie in God, and amongst them selues, wherfore, that religion is truest, that hath best meanes for vnitie of iudgment.

The Protestant, grounding his faith and proceeding vpon his owne spirit, (which he allwaies presumeth, but neuer proueth to be of the Lord) and euery man hauiug a spirit of his owne, must needes also haue a faith; & proceeding of his owne, wherin, if any other agree with him it is but by chaunce, sith that no two of them

A 4   ground

ground one conceipt vpon one & the
selfe same reason : for though Luther
and Caluin doe both deny transub-
stantiation , yet not vpon the same
ground. But Luther because his spirit
telleth him there is cōpanacion, that
is to say, both the flesh of Christ and
bread: and Caluin because his spirit
telleth him there is no corporall presence of Christ, nor anie thing at all
besides bread, but forceth a figure ; &
therfore about this, Luther & Caluīs
spirits doe mortallie iarre, werfore a-
mongst them it is not possible to haue
vnitie of faith, as also neuer wil be a-
mongst English Protestantes & Puritanes, because euerie mans owne spirit is the vncontrolable vmpier in all
doubts of faith, & apparteth it selfe
from each other.

The Catholiques wil be found all
to beleeue alike the same pointes of
faith, and to proceede all alike in the
sub-

substance of Gods seruice, and herein be in great vnitie, grounding all
that they beleeue, and doe, vpon one
and the selfe same reason, to wit vpon
obediéce due vnto the spirit of Christ
which is in his body the Catholique
church, whose publique iudgment
being once knowne, euery man con-
formeth (in cótrouersies) his iudgmét
therto, in vniformity of beliefe and
proceeding, and to knowe certainlie
the churches publique iudgment in
doubtes, only the catholiques haue a
most fit meane, by the knowne cósent
of all rhe pastors of euery particular
church in the world professed in general councels, where the head and
members doe meete in *Spiritu sancto*
(by mutual intelligence of them who
haue *clauem scientiæ* the key of knowledge, and offer to teach alwaies the
same doctrine which from their ance-
stours & ordainers they receiued without

o ut any iotte of alteration, by newe
fetch of witt or pretence of priuate
illumination in matters of faith : and
to propounde vnto their particular
flockes throughout the Chriftian
world thofe doctrines of faith, the o-
riginalls wherof, all antiquitie being
ript vp to finde out, their firft fountaine and fpring, are found to be
thofe reuelations which Chrift made
to his Apoftles, to be deriued to al po-
fterities by ordinary fucceffiue paftors
(as alwaies yet they haue beene and
fhall be) euen to the laft man that fhal
bee brought to Chriftes faith in the
end of the world.

3   The third vndoubted truth is,
That the Gofpell and true faith is the
power of God efficatio⁹ for mans faluation to conuert infidels, and bring
them to Chrift. That faith then is
truer, which hath conuerted more nations, and which is better furnifhed
                                    with

with powerful meanes to brig worldly wise men to chriſtianitie, wherfore
by this wee may ſee, wheather Catholiques, or Proteſtants faith be better,

The Proteſtants did neuer conuert
any Infidel nation to Chriſt, & ſome
of them wil ingenuouſlie cōfeſſe, that
though ſome few doe now and then
ſlip from the profeſſion of the olde
faith to their parte, yet, that no man
who was once throughly grounded
in the olde faith, came euer after to be
a ſound proteſtant, but rather careles
of God, & ſeemed zealous for faſhion
only, and deſignement. Neither doth
a Proteſtants onlie ground (to wit,
firſt his ſpirit, and then ſuch ſillables
and ſenſe of the Bible as it pleaſeth
him to admit for Gods word) affoord
him any motiue, fit to alter a prudent
moral man, who is an Infidel & ſtandeth vpon the light of nature, and the
vſe of his aunceſtours : wil the Proteſtant

ſtant bring to the Pagan a Bible? this
the Pagan eſteemes as we doe of the
Alcaron, to be a fardell of falſhoodes
and follies, and how can he conuince
a Pagan that his Bible is Gods truth?
will he tell the Pagan that he is the
miniſter of the Lord ſent to preach
the truth? The Pagan will aske to ſee
his commiſſion, and becauſe Chriſtians were ſaid to worke miracles, the
pagan will deſire to ſee a miracle, or a
proofe, that this fellow is the ordinary ſucceſſour (in chardge & vnformity
of doctrine) of thoſe Apoſtles, which
are ſaid to haue wrought miracles, in
confirmation of their calling and doctrine, for the cōuerſion of the world,
wherin this miniſter will be found to
faile. But if this miniſter doe vnfold
vnto him his owne pointes of prote-
ſtancy, that a chriſtian hath no fre-
dome of will to doe good, no power
in him ſelfe to refuſe ill, no reward for
wel-

wel-liuing, no disfauour with God for bad life, if he doth beleeue aright, but that a Christian may be a boare for lechery, a woolfe for cruelty, almost a lucifer for pride, & yet by only faith be a good christian. Surely the Pagan wil think Christianitie to be the most notorious abuse of nature and abhomination that may be. And yet the Protestant can say nothing else of his owne, to persuade Christianitie, of more substance, or more côformable to the groundes of his owne persuasion, then what I haue here put downe.

On the contrary side, none but Catholiques did euer worke the conuersion of nations, which is a signe that to them was giuen that commission. *Math.* 28. *Eûtes docete omnes gêtes,* going teach al natiôs, I am with you al daies euen to the consummation of the world: that with them is. *Lex Domini imma*

immaculata conuertens animas , that immaculate faith , that vnspotted law of
God , which (as the Prophet Dauid
saith) is a conuerter of soules. And
becaufe the Catholique knoweth,
that an intelligent and iudicious Infidel wil require of his Catachift , or
teacher , some prudét motiues of cre-
dulity (as reasonablie he may) that
he may prudently resolue vpon an al-
terarion of his religion, and prudence
may accompany his credulitie , to the
right information of his reasonable
soule. Therfore to this effect the Catholique wil by the order of the world
show, that God hath a prouidence &
gouernment, & consequétly he hath
prouided for man a religion, which, e-
uen nature telleth vs is due from man
to God , wherfore sith a reasonable
má, oweth to God a religious seruice,
& becaufe man knoweth not, so fully
by his owne reasó, the nature of God,

as

as that he can come to knowe what it seruice befits him best, therfore that it is fit that we should haue a doctrin e of religion reuealed : and then will h e proue that no reuealed doctrine is so credible as the Christian Chathol i- ques is, for being most agreable to na- ture in exalting God, and informing man to vertue. No so perfect a disp o- sition of any comon-wealth, as is the Catholique church, nor any peo ple so powreful in supernatural prero ga- tiues, as be the Catholique christia ns: and to this end he wil bring forth (be- sides olde prophecies which our e ne- mies the Iewes acknowledge to h aue beene before Christ, and are acc om- plished in the Catholique churc he) The miracles, the martir domes, the Anachorites, the virginities, the i no- nasticall institutions, their penitential liues in watching, fasting, praying, contemplation, how in great aboun-

dance

dance of temporalities, by abstinence
they pinche them selues, that by hos-
pitalitie they may be charitable to o-
thers, the authoritie and orderly continued hierarchy or holy order of suc-
cessiue pastours, & inferior orders of
the clergie, their learning, grauitie
and gouernment, the means of consent & vnitie of faith, iudgment, and
proceeding, amongst so many milli-
onf of millions as Christians are, and
haue beene, being of so diuers nations, customes, policies, & conditions,
the multitude, wisedome, victorious-
nes, and piety of princes and peoples,
which for almost this sixtenhundred
of yeares haue beene of the Catholique christian church.

These and many more arguments
of the supernaturall vocation of the
christians, which can not procede but
from God, and are found to bee allwaies amongst onlie catholique christians

ftians, may the catholique fubftanti-
ally proue out of vncontrowlable re-
cordes which cannot but moue a prudent infidel to think at leaft that chriftianitie is an eminent profeffion, and
though maruelous for the matters
beleeued, yet for the arguments in it,
that it commeth from God, worthy
of a reafonable mans beleefe. And
indeed who but God can be thought
to haue conuerted the wife and fen-
fual world, fo generally, and continually to fubmit their reafon to faith,
and the brauenes of their mindes, to
the humilitie of Chrift, and to tye
their fences to the afperities of the
croffe, by the only doctrine of a poore
crucified and cotemned man, whom
fome dozen bafe and vnlearned men
his companions preached to be God,
and them felues his meffengers to in-
ftruct the worlde.

4 The fourth truth is, that God be-

B   came

became man, and died, to redeeme to
him ſelfe, out of the maze and multitude of the impious worlde, a choice
people, who by his grace ſhould ſanctifie them ſelues, and be followers of
good workes, to which end true faith
was ordained as an eſpeciall and neceſſary meane: wherfore that faith is
Chriſts, that yeeldeth more meanes
of purity in conſcience, and conuerſation. See therfore wheather the Catholique or proteſtant religion indu-
ceth more purity of ſoule, and meanes
to auoide ſinne.

The Proteſtāts doctrine is, that man
hath no free will to doe good; nor
force of Gods grace, ſupporting and
enabling realy his ſoule to ouercome
temptations: that Gods children of
their good deeds done by the grace
of God haue no merit, that our beſt
workes are deadlie ſinnes, that a chriſtian mans iuſtice is comprized in the
only

only faith, and apprehension, that to him selfe (being a dánable síner & remaining abhominable in very deed) Chriftes iuftice is imputed; and that this once had, can neuer be loft, and whiles it is had, a man can not damne him felfe, be he neuer fo outragious in al filthy, bloodly, and cryinge finnes, euen til his laft breath : yea, Caluin is noted to teach, and detefted for it of very Lutherans them felues, (in that part not fo far gone) that God is the author of finne : which doctrine is not only blafphemous to God-warde, and iniurious to nature, but alfo infectious to al focieties of life, and ciuil conuerfation : for out of this it followeth, that Dauid was as iuft in his adultery of *Befarbe* and homicide of *Vrias*, as in his *penance*, and *miferere*; fith he had equally faith in both difpofitiõs, which he could not loofe by fuch lewdnes; wherfore, fith that by

the

the Proteſtantes doctrine, wil to doe
well, I can not: and doe ill, I muſt
needes: ſith good workes be improfi-
table, & bad deeds vndammadgable,
and to doe as God commandeth, is
meerely impoſſible: ſith my iuſtice by
only faith is had, and by any my fault,
but infidelitie, can not be loſt. VVhy
ſhould I a Proteſtant forbeare the
ſweet that is in al kind of ſinnes? why
ſhould I not ſeeke to aduantadge my
contentment in gluttonies, lecheries
reuendges, rapines, and treaſons? ſith
my iuſtice before God is ſolifidian, in-
dependent of my behauiour. So that
if I haue wit inough to doe il cloſe-
ly, or force inough to doe it freely in
reſpect of politique lawes, with God,
my faith ſecureth mee in the next
life of abſolute impunity for what-
ſoeuer villany: why then ſhould I Proteſtant goe about an impoſſible ab-
ſtinence from the ſweet of ſinne, this
                                      for

forbearance being so much contrary
to my sense, and so litle commodious
to my soule?

The Catholiques teach that a man
may if he will, and ought to keepe
Gods cōmandemētes, which though
to an immoderate & beastlie appetite
they be hard, yet to a reasonable man
regenerated in Christ, and fortified
with grace (had by merit of his blessed passion and meanes of his sacraments) they be a very sweete yoke and
a light burthen: that though the holie
faith of a Christian, and true knowledge of the mistery of Christ, be a
most excellent guift of God, yet that
it alone sufficeth not to christian iustice, but that a faithfull mans iustice
principally dependeth vpon his charitie towards God, his owne soule, &
his neighbour: & that not only Gods
lawes are to be kept vnder paine of
hel, but also the lawes of princes, not

ſo much for awe of man, as for conſcience towrrds God . That by the
merites of Chriſtes paſſion , we haue
grace & vertues inherent in our ſoule,
which ſo bettereth our nature, & for-
tifieth our frailty; as that in time of
temptation, we be ſtronger then any
faction of our goſtly enemies , or any
conſpiracy of the fleſh , world, and
diuel againſt vs, which whoſo ouer-
cometh not, can not be ſaued, vnleſſe
God giue him new grace after his fal
to doe true penance, & perſeuer in it,
that at the end of his life , death may
finde him either an innocent, or a pe-
nitent. The Catholiques teache that
Chriſtes precious death was ſo beneficial vnto vs, as that the merit therof
doth giue vs grace, wherby , not only
our ſinnes are remitted , & our ſoules
truly clenſed , but alſo we are truly
made the children of God, enabled
to worke ſuch good works, as for that
                                        graces

graces fake, (wherein the children of God are acceptable to their father) our workes doe merit the inheritance of the kingdome of heauen : God fo efteeming the roote of our worke : (to wit) his owne grace, which was bought for vs by the precious blood of Chrift, & conueyed into our foules from his croffe by his facramentes, as by fupernatural conduites.

The Catholiques teach, that we be fed with that felfe fame glorious body of our Sauiour Chrift, which fitteth at the right hand of God in heauen, not in a figure, or by fanta- fticall faith, but in very truth : wher-fore, it is to vs a great motiue and meane of purity in life, and charitie towards Chrift; an incentiue to me-ditate, and immitate his paffion; a fure pledge of eternall bliffe, that in this life he will haue not only our foules the temples of his fpirite, but alfo our

bodies

bodies the mansion of his most sacred flesh, so admirably effecting his bodylie abode continually with vs, which he affecteth as himselfe, expressed when he said. *Delitiæ meæ esse cum filiis hominū.* My delight is to be with the sonnes of men Besides the former meanes, motiues, and bonds to purity Catholiques doe teache vs, how that we be armed against the wicked spirits, by the protection of our guardian Angels & patronage of blessed soules: and to withstand the prouocation of our owne flesh, by cōsidering the presence of our iudge, by the memorie of our owne deathes, the iudgment we are going to, the eternall retribution of heauen if we conquer, of hel fire if we be ouercome: and withall, to chastise that with discreet paines, which doth entice vs to fond delightes: & to oppose to the ill examples of naughty worldlings, the memory how Christ

and

and his faincts conuerſed in this world,
ſtriuing againſt ſinne euē til death. To
conclude, ſuch abſtinences, retirings,
prayings, watchings, and other afflictions of our fleſhe, as diſcreetly and
profitably be vſed amongſt Catholiques, ſuch often pure cōfeſſions, prouiſion againſt recidiuation, exhorta-
tions, and care of ghoſtly ſuperiors,
obedience, and awe both of God and
man, in ſubiects, and inferiours, ſuch
inſtitutions of religious orders, ſuch
diſcipline to mortifie our wilde de-
ſires, and auoid occaſions of ſlippes to
ſinne : in al thinges, ſuch helpe of Sacraments, & other graces of the holie
Ghoſt (which is working in the children of the catholique church alone)
how can it but breed great puritie in a
man that hath any deſire to doe well ?

5 The fift vndoubted truth is. That
true religion being a due, which as
nature teacheth all men we owe to
God,

God, true faith is reuealed by God to man, to direct and ſettle him in the vſe of his religion towards God, both in in-ward piety, and outward ceremony of externe homadge and worſhip. VVherfore that faith of new or olde is better, that doth more direct and ſettle a man in inward Deuotion, and that outward church ſeruice, which was alwaies vſed among chriſtians.

True religion conſiſting of two eſpecial parts: wherof one is in ward deuotion, and the other outward worſhip, by externe ceremonies: for the firſt, to wit inward deuotion, we muſt firſt note, that as other vertues may be fained, ſo may deuotion alſo: yea, a man may miſtake himſelfe to be deuout, when he is not ſo. Secondlie we muſt remember the diſcourſe of S. Paul: *Rom:* 10. who affirming that a right prayer is a ſpeciall meane to ſaluation,

uation, putteth thefe interrogatories. But *hovv* (faith he) *shal they call on him, in vvhome they haue not beleeued? and hovv shall they beleeue in him, of vvhome they haue not heard? and hovv shall they heare, vvithout a preacher? and hovv shall they preache, vnles they be sent?* Hitherto S. Paul, as if he fhould fay, no miffion, no preacher; no preacher, no catechifinge; no catechifinge, no beleefe; no beleefe no true inuocation; and confequently no inward deuotion.

It being proued then out of S. Paul here cited, that the notice that can be had of the true inuocation, and inwarde true deuotion of the people, muft be had, by the certaine notice had of the miffion, and lawfull calling of their paftours, (whofe preaching is the ordinary meane to that true faith which is neceffary to true deuotion) how can the proteftant (who is carelefe of the lawfull calling of his

his preacher) prudétly perfuade him-
felfe, that he praieth as he ought with
true deuotion, more then a Iewe, or a
Turke doth? both which mifcreants
doe feeme more zealous, and deuout,
then our proteftants; or the nature of
chriftianitie beinge fuche, that the
fpecialleft externe motiue to it, is the
certaine miffion of Chrift from his
father; of his Apoftles, from him; of
other Paftours fucceffiuely, frô them;
through generation and generation
to the end of the worlde; which is
the reafon wherfore, both, Chrift and
his Apoftles, and their fucceffours doe
firft of all cleare this pointe, that they
haue a lawfull miffion to preache
truth : it being withall demonftrable :
(which the minifters know well i-
noughe, and therfore ftil feeke to a-
uoid this queftion. *Quis te mifit?* who
fent thee?) that the proteftant minifter hathe no lawfull miffion to teach
                                his pro-

his proteſtancie; all this (I ſay) being true in it ſelfe, and well conſidered of vs, how can it be poſſible to thinke that a Proteſtant faith can bring true inward deuotion?

The ſeconde part of religion is outward worſhipe, a ſpecial portion wherof, alwaies as yet ſince the creation of the world til now, externe ſacrifice was counted, and was alwaies vſed in Gods church.

The proteſtants haue aboliſhed all ſacrifice, preiſthoode, and altar, and codemned of ſuperſtition all church-ſeruice, that is knowne to haue bene in vſe in Gods church through-out the worlde, euer ſince Chriſt, euen till this day: ſo that wheras the law of nature ſince Adam, had alwaies ſome truly ſeruig God in due externe worſhipe, til the ſinagogue began: & that had alwaies ſome true worſhippers, euen till Chriſt: Chriſt him ſelfe hath beene

beene without true worshipe at al, in his church seruice, (as the Protestants doe teach) euen til rhis day, superstition raigning in euery parte of Christendome. Now wheather that the Protestāts common praier booke be void of superstition or no, let the Puritan iudge by the scriptures, and wheather the Puritans conuenticles be according to the worde, let the familists, superilluminats, & the Brownists iudge by the wotd and spirite.

The Catholiques externe motiue to faith is the authority of the allwaies-visible christian churche : of whome Christ sald. *As my father sent me, so send I you:* and confirmed their mission with miracles. And therfore the Catholiques be most prudentlie certaine of the churches mission, and consequently of the truth of their owne faith, wheron their inward deuotion is founded.

As

As for externe homadge : the catholiques folowinge Chriftes inftitution,
& the deuoute vfe of all their aunce-
ftor-chriftians, haue for their church-
feruice that pure facrifice, and oblation, prefigured in *Melchifidech*; and by
Malachi fo longe before prophecied
of: to wit, the vnblody facrifice of the
moft facred bodie & precious bloode
of Chrift, now dailie on the altar in
the churche offered by the miniftery
of Gods priefts, in continual memory of Chriftes bloody facrifice, once
offred on the croffe for our ful redép-
tion, therby daily to apply vnto vs the
merits of Chrifts death : and withall,
to giue vs an earneft and pledge of life
euerlafting: and this is done with fuch
facred rites, and folemne ceremonies,
as Gods fpirit in the firft paftours of
Chrifts church knew was moft feemly
and fit to mainteine deuotion and reuerence to God, in Chriftian harts,
wher-

wherfore, if certainty, vnitie, purity
of soule, if efficacy to conuert sinners,
inward deuotion, & the constant vse
of Church seruice in Christianitie be
regarded of you, (as in reason they
should) you shall see in what faith
these are founded, and how farre they
be from this new profession. For a
conclusion this I assure you by myne
owne, and other mens longe experience, that there is no man remaines a
protestant, if he once looke into the
groundes of religion, but such as continue doubtful, what faith to follow:
not for want of meanes to see truth,
but for feare that if they looke further into it, they should be conuinced
that only the catholique faith is true:
and consequently should forsake many
commodities, and sustaine many dis-
graces for that profession, or suffer a
sharper corasiue of conscience then
they did before, for practising against
so

so knowne a truth : like vnto those of whom the Prophet Dauid saith, *Noluit intelligere vt bene ageret* : and as it is written, *Lux venit in mundum, & dilexerunt homines tenebras magis , quam lucem.* Light came into the worlde, and men loued darknes more , then light: which I do hope, and will pray, that it may be farre from you.

Reasõs vvhy after due search I being once resolued, vvill admit no farther conference in Religion.

HAVING by Gods grace, & my parents care , beene so brought vp, that alwayes I had regard to mine owne saluation ; And hearing those of the olde and new religion, to differ so farre in doctrine of faith, (that faith which is true , being of all sides accounted necessary to saluatiõ) I durst

G   not

not die (and why fhould I liue fo as I dare not die) and come to that dreadfull iudgement, wherto now liuing I am paffing, if now in life I did not make diligent fearche in what faith to die, and what preachers to beleeue and obey in the gouernment of my life; efpecially feeing, that though Luther (the firft parent of the new preachers) doe damne to the pitt of hell, the facramentaries both Zuinglians and Caluinifts, and both thefe condemne his doctrine: yet almoft all thefe new preachers doe vniformely confent, that our forefathers liuing and dying in the olde religion, might for all that be faued; wheras they of the olde religion do côftantly affirme, & that with great côpaffion to them of whom they do fo fpeake, that thefe preachers of the new fafhion, haue quitt them felues and their followers from the means of eternall faluation,

by

1739507

by relying vpon that, as vpon faith, which is meere fancy and infidelytie, vsing the scriptures, sacraments, and stile of Christians for pompe, not for profit; for shew, not for saluation. VVhich being consered, I feare, least both before God I should be censured of impietie, & before man of folly, if I should not resolue, as all others of iudgement and good disposition doe, who consider these premises. To wit, that sith to both of these contradictory preachers I can not giue credit; and beleeue these, rather then those rashly, I may not: I should not, as one preiudiced by mine education amongst the new preachers, sitt still without thought of further searche, (sith mine owne ignorance, proceeding of such negligence, will not more excuse me before God, if I doe therfore erre, then ignorance will excuse him, who hath meanes to come out of his er-

C 2 rour

rour, wherin he was bred & brought
vp, amõgst Turcks or Heathẽs, Iewes
or Arrians;) But before I vnreafona-
blelie addict my felf to any fide, without fuch proofe of fpirits, as befemeth
me, in this my litle skill of Gods matters: Firft by humble prayers, diligent
fearch, and beft aduife, by reading of
bookes, efpecially in fuch points, as be
generall grounds of other controuer-
fies, I will indeuour to find out thofe
preachers, to whome I might iuftly
giue credit in a matter of fuch importance , as is true faith , the firft
meane to eternal bliffe. Remembring
alwayes, that as Gods creature , I owe
to my creator a feruice, worfhip, and
reuerence: and as a reafonable creature, a reafonnable feruice, worfhip,
and reuerence: This reafon therfore,
that God hath giuen me I muft make
vfe of, to examine, to whome of thefe
contradictory preachers in matters of
faith

faith neceſſary to ſaluatiō I muſt yeeld my ſelf perſuaſible; that is to ſay, whether the motiues of prudence to yeeld an aſſent to the olde preachers, or to the new, be more grounded in true reaſon, all preiudice of affeçtion and partialitie to factions layd a ſide.

First of all then I do conſider, that two waies onely there be imaginable, wherby it is poſſible to take notice, whether the old or new preachers are to be beleeued; wherof the firſt is, by the knowledg obtained before hand of the truth of the doctrines (which they ſeuerally deliuer) allreadie gotten by mine owne induſtry, by which I may diſcerne, that theſe preachers rather then thoſe, are with greater reaſon to bee followed. The ſecond way how to know this, is, if before I doe penetrate their ſeuerall doctrins, I doe firſt find out, which rancke of theſe preachers be woorthy of moſt

C 3　　　　credit

credit and authoritie to be beleeued
in doctrines, as yet vnknowen to me:
and then to let my self, in the beginning of my searche of truth be moued
with that greater authoritie, which I
haue found to be more in one rancke
of preachers, then in an other, and
therby iudiciously to gather, that this
preacher teacheth truth, rather then
the other: allthough my selfe of my
selfe, doe not as yet perspicuously vnderstand the particular reason, why
that doctrine or article is most true,
which is taught by such a preacher, to
whome I prudently yeld my selfe a
disciple, because of his euident authoritie to teache mee.

Touching the former of these waies
of triall, wherby I may find out to
what preacher I may prudently ad-
here, or adioyne my selfe, that is to say,
by the foreknowledge which I haue
already gotten, particularly of euery
                                    doctrine

doctrine in cōtrouersy, amongst olde
and new diuines; Though they who
make true doctrine a note and signe
of the churche, wherunto I must render obedience , seeme to prescribe
this way : yet doth my conscience
witnesse, that to me (howsoeuer it be
in respect of others)this way is meerly
impossible: (and yet euen to mee likewise , God hath left some meanes of
saluation.) For I may not so farre o-
uer-weane my witt & learning, as to
thinck that I am able (no not after
some reading of bookes, and hearing
of opinions, much lesse at the beginning of my searche for truth) to lead
my selfe, without the authorytie of a
guide and directour , through the
depth of these disputes; & to pearce
into the nice points of euery difference , in positions of faith , betwixt the
olde and new preachers; when they
teache vs that wee must, or must not
beleeue

beleeue as our anceftours did; of the
manner of our iuftification by Chrift;
of the roote, & worth of thofe works
which are wrought by the children
of God; of the number, valew, and o-
peration of facraments; the effence,
& effect of originall finne; the precife
manner of Chrifts prefence in the
bleffed facrament; the releafe of temporall paines due to finns already remitted; *opus operatum*; works of coun-
faill, or fupererogated aboue and befides that which is neceffary to be
done, for the efcaping of hell fyer: &
a thoufand fuch like points fo intricate, that a ripe witt after much ftudy
cannot without diffyculty know directly, wherin the queftió lieth which
is debated : much leffe fhall I bee able
to poize, and weighe the proofes and
reproofes, replies, and anfweres, du-
plications, & triplications, reprehen-
fions, and reioynders, wherwith the
greateft

greateſt clarks of our age, haue filled
the world; euery one ſeeking ſo to in-
ſtance, and anſwer his aduerſary, as
that the worlde is now after all this
a-doe, more cloyed with wrangling
contradictions in particular controuerſies; but ſimple & vnlearned men
not more edified with fitter inſtructi-
ons to true chriſtianitie, then before
theſe diſputes began. As for my ſelfe
(not to ſpeake of other greater witts)
I cãnot thinck that God doth require
of one of my ſort, that I ſhould bee a
conſummate maiſter of diuinitie, before I be a puney ſcholar of the true
church, as I muſt needs bee, if I will
take this way of triall of truth, firſt
rightly to cenſure by mine owne skill
in ſcripture, and mine owne priuate
iudgement, learned mens deciſions
in all particular controuerſies, and
therby to know what preachers to
follow.

For

For mee therefore remaineth onely the second way, which I finde to my selfe possible, to the vse of all good christians of auncient times most cóformable, and in the iudgement of the latest and cunningest protestant writers, seemeth most commendable: as appeareth by these words of M. Docteur Field, in his dedicatory, teaching, *That seeing the controuersies of religion in our age, are grovvne in number so many, and in nature so intricate, that fevv haue time & leasure, fevver strength of vnderstäding to examine them: nothing remaineth for men desirous of satisfaction in things of such consequence, but dilsgently to search out, vvhich amongst all societies of men in the vvorld, is that blessed company of holy ones, that houshold of faith, that spouse of Christ, and church of the liuing God, vvhich is the pillar, and ground of truth; that so they may embrace her communion, folovv her direction, and*
rest

rest in her iudgement. VVhich coūsayll of this protestant doctour, seemeth to bee very iudicious, and of mee, who desire a prudent satisfaction in controuersies of religion, to be imbraced: as it is also of all wise and iudicious persons, by M. Fields report, who saith in the same place. *That hence it comes, that all vvise and iudicious men doe more esteeme bookes of doctrinall principles, then those that are vvritten of any other argument: and that there vvas neuer any treasure houlden more rich, then bookes of praescriptions against the profane nouelties of heretiques: For that therby men that are not vvilling or not able, to examine the infinite differences, that arise amongst men concerning the faith, haue generall directions, vvhat to follovv, and vvhat to auoide.* Thus farr M. Doctour Field, in his said dedicatory, graced by my Lord of Conterbury, and therfore more to be respected of any protestãt.

By

By All which, hauing now found out, both in the vſe of the olde preachers, and in the doctrine of the new, that the onely prudent way to ſearch for Gods truth is, firſt by finding out what company of preachers bee of moſt authoritie : and then by their authoritie, to be led at firſt into the notice of particular doctrines : My next care is to conſider, wherupon authoritie riſeth ; and heere I ſee, that men come to authoritie, either by much eſteemed guiftes, & good parts of nature and induſtry, fit to winne credit amongſt wiſe men ; as the witt, ſtudy, nobilitie, multitude, antiquitie, honeſt conuerſation, and ſuch like commendable parts, knowne to be in any company, or church, which maketh this or that profeſſiõ : or elſe the authoririe of preachers of a religion, proceedeth of the ſupernaturall priuiledges ſeene in them, which they

can

cannot haue had, but from heauen, as diuine prerogatiues, exceeding all humane forces; and bee worthy signes, that those men be sent from God, to instruct the world; And of these sorts of supernaturall causes of credit and authoritie be; the working of miracles, knowen and tried patience in martyrdome, or perfect cōtempt and renouncing of the world, orderly succession into the offices, and doctrines of olde pastours : with other such like, as were seene in Chrifts Apostles, and their disciples, who neither vsurped place of pastours, nor altered doctrine of faithe.

Cōparing then the olde preachers with the new, in such good parts and priuiledges from God, both naturall and supernaturall, which may make them duely to be regarded, as persons of authority, worthy to be followed in matters of saluation : I shall thinke
that

that I haue per formed in this behalfe
my duty before God, & all good men,
jf after this comparison wisely made
& the odds seene, which are betwene
the new and olde: I doe submitt my
soule to them, whose authoritie I
fynde to be greater.

Yf then we examine discretely,
wheather in the old or new preachers
there be more causes of credit, & authority: surely the causes of credit
and authoritie duely considered, (first
wayghing the difference of naturall
meanes of credit) we should too much
wrong the memory of our forefathers, and our owne experience, and
due censure of our owne dayes, if
we should imagin that Luther, or Caluin, or any such new reuolter frō the
olde faith, which before times them
selues had longe professed, to a conceipt of their owne coyning; & from
that laudable chastitie, and penitēn-
tiall

tiall life, which them selues had for a longe time, bothe professed, and pretended to obserue, vnto a course of notorious sensualitie, & vntamed lust: if we shoulde (I say) imagine that either them selues, or their followers are to be preferred before our auncestours; these new ministers being indeed so new, so few, so lewdly reported of one by an other; not elder then the age of three or foure score yeares, not spred farther then three or foure Northren prouinces, into certaine corners; whither they are come, by open force, and knowne fraudulence: wherin they lye scattered heere and there, amõgst the basest sorte & rudest peoples: hauing seized vpon none besides those, who bee of weaker iudgements, and stronger appetites, and do seeme in the fashion of their life least carefull of christian cõuersation. VVherfore these new preachers can

not

not possiblie be so auncient in continuance, so great in number, so reue-
rend for wisdome, of so ripe iudgement, or so skilfull in learning, more
prudēt in coūsaill, grauer of manners,
more exemplar in conuersation, then
were and are the old preachers, who
no sooner knew, then cōdemned this
new faith, they hauing flourished for
so many ages and centuries of yeares,
as haue beene since Christ: and that
in all christian nations ouer the face
of the earth; in the communion of so
many wise & worthy princes, and prelates; such graue and vertuous people
and cōmonwealthes, so commended
to our imitation, and example, as pa-
ternes of true wisedome, bothe in publique and priuate affaires; in such
meanes, & encouragements, to piety,
and learning, by errections of mona-
steries, and endowments of colledges
preferments for well-deseruers, re-
gular

gular inftitutions of moft chriftian
difcipline: the monuments of whofe
pietie, wifdome, and knowledge be
fo manifeft, that all our prouifions for
publique good & learned woorks in
diuine and humane knowlege, were
the fruits of their religious labours.

But if we looke to fupernaturall
caufes of authoritie, by which, God
doth with fpeciall affiftãce priuiledge
thofe, to whom he will giue the office
and authoritie of true preachers of
his will and worde in this worlde; we
fhall yet fee farr more excelléce in the
old preachers then in the uew, or (to
fay the truth) all in the old, and none
in the new. For either all records of
antiquity, ftories of times, courtrolls
of corporations, publique and vncon-
trollable relations both auncient and
moderne, do faile of truth, as made of
purpofe to deceiue good minds : or
elfe the preachers of the old religion
D
with

with their people doe most iustly
challenge as their owne possession,
continued since Christes ascension,
the ordinary succession of hierarchie
by Christ ordained then, and established to endure till the worldes end, to
the saluation of all nations; all miracles wrought for the effectuall per-
formance of conuerting all Christian
nations : all the christians martyr-
doms suffered till this day; all the san-
ctity of confessours, chastity of virgins, deuotion of matrones, the pe-
nitentiall life of conuerted sinners; in
a worde all the glory which Christ
hath hitherto had, or yet hath as the
fruit of his blessed passion in his
churche militant; VVheras this new
factiō of preachers, disclaimeth from
the power of doinge miracles, defieth
ordinary pastours and pastourship,
thincking themselues to be extraor-
dinarily raised, without any proofe of
their

their miſſion : and for their holynes
of life, they whome they counte the
beſt of their confederates, haue no o-
ther perfections, then were and may
be now founde in Pagans , hauing
much a doe to finde their moſt refor-
med miniſtrie matcheable with ordinary artizans in forbearig from groſſe
crimes, & crying ſinnes in worde and
work ; witnes wherof be euery aſſizes,
ſeſſions, and particular pariſhes, wherin though many of the miniſters dis-
orders be huſht vp for glory of the
Ghoſpell, and neuer come to triall:
yet the propoſition of number of miniſters and other men being conſidered, the knowne miſdemeanure, diſ-
ſentions and heynous crimes of the
miniſters, are farr more then thoſe of
the cōmon people : wheras their doctrine being ſo lately ſprung vp, and
yet but in the feruour & flour, ſhould
at leaſtwiſe for ſome ſmall time haue

brought

brought forth in the preachers therof fruits of greater pietie, vnion, and
charitie; which are found moft abundantly afrer fo many ages, if not in all,
yet in the moft eminent, and greater
part of efteemed and renowned preachers, in writters, and profeffours of
the olde religion. Befides thefe new
preachers make a ieft at virginitie &
a cōtinent life, not abiding the name
of penance, and conceiting of Gods
fweet will and commandements, as
of meere impoffibilities : which doctrine in it felfe, opening the way to
licentioufnes, and giuing fo large an
excufe of not liuing well, as of a thing
impoffible; how can the profeffours
therof be thought, to haue any care
of holyneffe or good life?

To this we may add iuftly, that thefe
new preachers doe not vfe their pul-
pits and prints, as ftriuing to edifie either vertue in cōuerfation, or pofitiue

points

points in doctrine, more then in auncient times (which yet they should
doe, if, as they professe, they performe
the office of teachers more faithfully
then the olde preachers) but they specially bende all their forces to destroy
what they founde before them built,
as though it were a sufficient sauinge-
faith , not to bee of the catholique
Romane faith; though otherwise no
small errours in principall points of
saluation be admitted, or wincked at,
and permitted. Neither could I euer
see any iust motiue in our new preachers proceedings, by which a prudent heathen man, no grosse idolater,
(as many haue been in time of idola-
try) might be conuerted from that
kinde of seruice, and acknowledging
the God of nature alone, which his
aunceftours did teach him , to cōfesse
the diuine misteries of the christian
faith, being so farre aboue reason, and

therfore necessarily relying vpon authoritie seene and acknowledged in
the preachers; Nor why the new preacher of any sect be it Lutheran, Sa-
cramétary; Anabaptist, or Trinitary?
should moue a man, whom he would
seduce from the old faith to his owne
sect, rather then to any others of these
new sects, or old heresies of all that
rable of errours, which haue troubled
the catholique church from Simon
Magus, to Iohn Caluin or Michael
Seruethus, Sith all old heretique and
new teachers, though among them
selues each one most aduersary to o-
thers, in their speciall doctrines, do
preténd the selfe same grounds of faith,
to witt, what pleaseth them to call
Gods word, both in syllable & sence.

But a man may see very greate cause
giuen by these new ministers proceedings, why many in our dayes drawne
from the catholique faith by Calui-
nisme

nifme, come to Arianifme and Tri-
theifme, and fuch monfterous fects,
from which they fall backe into Iu-
daifme, or into the originall blindnes
of corrupted nature, from acknowledging any miftery at all of the chriftian faith: as Bucerus, and Ochinus,
and other fuch doctours are certainly
known to haue done, falling from catholiques to be Sacramétarie: wherby hauing left the firme foundation
of all Chriftianity, to witt, the authoritie of that churche, which is called
by S. Paul the pillar & groud of truth
and vfing no other armes againft Pa-
piftrie (as they call it) thē thofe which
a Pagan may vfe againft all Chriftianitie, no maruaill that hauing loft
their footinge in Gods church, without which, the vnderftanding cannot
ftay in chriftianitie, their tumbling
vagrát wittes runne headlong into A-
theifme; as befides others, *Iordanus*

D 4   *Brunus*

Brunus did, who once a friar, after an
Apoftata, firft from his order, then
from catholique religion, laftly from
Chrift, after he had bene a profeffour
in oxford, hauing tried all new fects,
and taried in none, was for obftinacy
in fuch Atheifme hanged in Rome.
Anno 1600.

It being then before neceffarily re-
folued, that in this important matter
of my foule, I muft deale prudently;
and prudence teaching mee that in
points of faith I muft yield my felfe
difciplinable, to be inftructed by thofe
preachers, who be of greateft authority, cauſed by naturall and fupernaturall good partes and graces, founde
in the preachers of a religion: I hope
that neither God will condemne me
of infidelity, nor wife men of folly,
nor good people of impiety, if I do
adheare, and cleeue to the preachers
of the old religion, as to the true paftours

stours sent from God for my instruction.

Yf after all this reason allredy giuen
of my doubt, search, and resolution:
I shal be still moued to admitt furrher
conference in more particular manner : then must I recurre to that protection, who did *appoint* and *direct* and
louingly accept and *fauorably approue* M.
Field booke, to which in this point
my proceeding shal be most conformable. *VVe admitt*) saith M. Doctor
Field in his preface or epistle dedicatory to my L. of Canterbury) *No man*
(*saith Tertullian in his book of prescripti-*
ons) *to any disputation concerning sacred*
and diuine things, or the scanning & exa-
mining of particular questions of religion :
vnlesse he first-shevv vs of vvhom he re-
ceaued the faith, by vvose means he be-
came a christian, and vvhether he admitt
and holde the generall principles, vvherin
all christians doe, and euer did agree : other-
vvise

vvise prescribing against him as a straun-
ger from the commonvvealth of the Israel
of God, and hauing no part nor felovvship
in this businesse. Thus farre M. Filed,
who in accepting from Tertullian, &
commending to vs this rule, is by authoritie approued, & therfore for pra-
ctizing of this rule, I hope I shall not
be condemned, if conformably to it,
before I doe admit further coference
in matter of faith, I humbly and simply craue, to haue this first cleared, to
witt, of whom that man, (with whom
I shalbe vrged to conferr about faith)
hath receaued his faith : that is to say,
wheather from some authour of nouelties, arising against his knowne pa-
stour; or from such as can deriue his
pastourship & doctrine by succession
throughe all ages, from the Apostles
to these our dayes : by whose meanes
he came to be a christian; and wheather he doe admitt and holde the generall

nerall principles, in which all Christians doe, and euer did agree? VVhich
interrogatories till they be satisfied, I
may not admitt conference by worde
or writing with any man in points of
faith, but by this approued rule must,
till thē, hold him as an alien from the
Israel of God: and as one that hath no
part in writting or speaking about the
busines of christianity.

Neither lett any man rashly thincke,
that to those, who will needs cōferre
with me, these interrogatories are
needlesse: sith my doubts heerin be
not either peeuish, or vnreasonable,
but most aduised and iust. For what
reason or authoritie haue I to thincke
that God hath vsed any meanes to
bring the now-christians of England
to the faith, other then his ordinary
course appointed in the beginning by
hearing of Chrifts worde, inuiolably
kept, and immutably preached by a
pa-

a paſtour of knowne miſſion and authoritie, ſucceſſiuely through all generations: with lawfull ordination &
iuriſdiction, deriued to him from the
Apoſtles of Chriſt, in whome only,
Chriſt by ordinary courſe doth ſpeake? and ſith we doe plainly ſee this
matter of fact, to witt, that the beginning and progreſſe of our new preachers manner of proceeding, and
dogmatizing, is againſt the ordinary
authority and receaued doctrine, of
the allwayes knowne & viſible chriſtianitie: and that they doe relye, not
vpon the olde and always-vnited ſuc-
ceſſion of paſtours, and vniforme doctrine, but vpon a priuate, new, and
rebellious ſeperation from both, and
therfore in the eye of any prudét man,
though he were no chriſtian, their
partialitie and profeſſion is to be accounted of as a latter and particular
faction, newly deuided from the an-
cient

cient chriftians, as the Perfian Mahometan is now reputed a fehifmaticall
Mahometan, lately aparted from the
former knowne profeffours of that
falfe religion of Mahomet. This y fay
being moft cleare to any one, that
for his foules health vouch-fafeth to
looke vnto it: how many iuft caufes
haue I to doubt, that this new faction
of profeffours, vnder the name of
chriftianity were not made chriftians
by the ordinary paftours? And therfore Tertullians prefcription, with
M. Fields approbation, and my L. of
Conterburies acceptation, may very
well ouerrule me to take exceptions,
and prefcribe againft them, that I a
catholique may refufe their conference in faith, till they haue firft cleared thefe interrogatories by fuch proper and direct anfwers, as be peculiar
to the true Chriftians indeed, and no
wayes appliable to the vfe of euery fe-
ctary,

ctary, aswell to be Brownist, Anabaptist, or Arrian, as to the Proteftant, or
Puritan: who all will, and with equall
truth may fay, that they had their
faithes and fantafies out of the fcripture, acknowledged and expounded
by their owne fpirits.

Moreouer, if I be vrged to conferre, with a minifter (as it is likely I
fhall,) then after the former interrogatories, I muft craue a furthei refo-
lution from him, (before I admitt him
for my Maifter in faith, as he will no
doubt pretend to bee) about the nature and quality of his miffion, and
authority, iurifdiction, and Paftourfhip. For it being out of controuerfy,
by plaine fcriptures, that no man can
preach vnleffe he be fent; & that therfore Chrift came fent, and fo he fent
others wit h p wer of fpirit, in miraculous workes, and holy liues, mani-
fefting their authority and calling to
                                        be

be preachers; and that the paftours of Chriftes erection at his afcenfion, muft be the men, who fhall call and keepe in chriftianity all the whole world, till the day of iudgement ; That Chrift did alfo forwarne vs of extraordinary commers vnfent, though they preted to be fent in his name ; As alfo that neuer any true preacher yet was fent from God extraordinariiy to bring in a new religion, diuers from the vfe of his aunceftours, but he came furnifhed with the power of miracles, to manifeft his power or paftourfhip, all this I fay being cleare by fcripture, how dare I anfwer God at the day of iudgement, for admittaunce of thefe minifters for my maifters in faith, and conferring with them in that manner, before it be manifeftly cleered vnto me, whence they are, and who fent them ? Efpecially fith that yet they can not agree among them felues,

whea-

wheather their firſt fathers miſſion &
Paſtourſhip was ordinary, or extraordinary: and both opinions appeare to
be meere deuiſes and colluſions; ſith
if it were extraordinary, by what rule
or exãple in ſcripture can they proue,
that they muſt bee taken for ſuch v-
pon their bare wordes, without miracles; or how do they proue that they
are not thoſe of whome Chriſt fore-
warnes vs, that would come in ſhew
as ſent, and yet indeed not ſent? But
if it was ordinary, ſurely by their doctrine, & as they blaſpheme the Pope,
(from whom in this opinion they pretend to haue it) it is meerly antichriſtian: ſo that now Chriſt is preached
truly by thoſe preachers onely, who
can ſhewe no patent of their commiſſion and authority of Paſtourſhip, but
onely vnder the broad ſeale of Antichriſt, and by conferring with them,
I ſhould be forced to learne my creed,

of

of Antichriſtian doctours.

After I ſhall haue receiued due ſatisfaction in my doubtes already pro-
pounded about my côference ; namely, how he became a chriſtian ; whether he holdeth the vniuerſall faith ;
and who ſent him to feed Gods flock:
becauſe the preſent Engliſh congregation is now, & was allwayes from the
beginning implacablely deuided into
two notorious factions (beſides the
ſeparation of Browniſts, and ſuch like
reformers) and was neuer more then
now out of hope of attonement in
them ſelues, one ſtill chardginge the
other with ſchiſme and rebellion, or
elſe with ſuperſtition, & perſecution
of the truthe : It ſtandeth me vpon to
know, wheather the party whome I
vrged to conferr withall, bee a puritane, or a proteſtant : not that their
proceeding will be much different in
ſyncerity: (for as we catholiques finde

E   in

in Iewell, and the protestants, misalle-
gations, reiections, and wresting of
scriptures and fathers from their true
wordes and sense, to make them serue
the Protestants meaning: so doe the
protestants abundantly obserue in the
puritanes writing against them: reade
but the protestants suruay of the puritanes discipline *chap.* 27. 36. 31. wherin at large this is plainly manifested)
but because the puritane conferrour
wil be sure to draw me towards puri-
tanisme, which (as theselues cofesse)
is held by those (whome I haue as
much reason to beleeue as them) to
be a *discipline dāned to hell from vvhence
it came:* and their doctrine is generally
called a *schisme*, and *heresy, treason*, and
rebellion; and the putitans *proclaimed to
be obstinate and refractarious persons, enemies to the king and state, notorious and
manifest schismatiques, false prophetes,
members rent and cutt of from the churche*

of

of God: &c. for more I am weary to write; which you may see in the silenced ministers challenge of cōference made to the prelates, dedicated to his majesty, printed. 1606. *pagin.* 9. and 10. And therfore till the Puritās haue freed themselues from these probable (as you may see in the protestant booke called *Dangerous positions , of Geneuites , scottizing* &c .) imputations, layd vpon them by men of greater authoritie then them selues, and more experienced in Puritan proccedings then I my selfe am , I can not with due respect to God , my prince, and country, thus conferre in religion with any purytane.

And as for the Protestant, being so publiquely & bitterly challenged and (if he will not accept the challenge) out dared by the puritane : he can neither with his owne honour , nor hope of altering me, fly the puritans field :

and

and pretend zeale in pressing me to
cóbat; Sith diuers of the propositions
(in approuing of which, except they
should be willfull traitours to God,
their prince, & country, they say that
they cánot but make opposition vnto
the Prélats *ibid. pag.* 16.) are such, as
if the ministers should not constantly
holde, and maintaine the same againft
all men : they cannot see how possi-
blely by the rules of diuinity, the se-
paration of our Proteftants church as
from the church of Rome, and from
the Pope the supreme head therof,
can be iuftified : yea promising their
reconcilement to that sea, if the Pa-
pifts can either by argumēts put them
from their forsaid propositions, or can
answer their arguments (thus they say
ibid. pag. 11.) for if the puritans be in
an errour, and the prelats on the contrary haue the truthe (they speake nothing of their yealding to the prelats,
                                    no,

no , no ,) *They protest to all the vvorlde,*
that the Pope and the church of Rome, & in
them, God and Christ Iesus himselfe haue
had great vvronge and indignitie offered
them, in that they are reiected , and all the
protestants churches are schismaticall , in
forsaking vnitie and communion vvith
them. ibid.pa.16. VVherby you see iust
reason why I may refuse the protestants conference : who if he be out
dared by the puritan, ought not to be
entertained by mee ; if he entring cōference with the Puritan , yeald vnto
him, then he is no more a protestant
but a puritan , against whom I haue
already taken iust exceptions : but if
he conquer the puritan , it is but by
that truth, which he borroweth from
vs, from the doctrine and practize of
our Church : and therfore both the
Puritan will in that case, and the Protestant ought to become as I am, a catholique.

E 3   More-

Moreouer, because not onely Protestants and puritans, but also Familists, and brownists, and each sectary
else (as it is certaine, and you may see
it proued in the protestants suruay of
the Puritans doctrine, (*cap*. 1.) doe
pretend zeale, and therfore will needs
vrge conference in place where they
preuaile : & seing that (of mine owne
knowledge) their wat not in England
eminent men, for magistracy, dignity,
and authority in the commonwelth,
who bee knowne familists, as also o-
ther some of markee which fauoure
Brownists, so that it may be my hape,
or some other catholiques to fall into
such hands as will vrge conference :
that we may receaue instruction in
these sectes; I would craue to know,
whether in that case I may entertaine
conference with a familist, or Brownist or no? If yea, what reason for it,
since these do detest the religion allo-
wed

wed by the state? if no, what reason,
sith these also show as great zeale of
Sion, teach with as great authoritie,
bring as much scripture, promise as
much truth, as the Protestants do?

Lastly, sith conference presuppo-
seth doubt, which my former search
hath excluded: and search must there
end, where satisfaction is founde:
wherefore should I search any more,
who now dare boldly answer the diuell in the houre of my death, & God
in the day of iudgement: that not the
presumption of mine owne witt, or
skill in scripture, nor any preiudice of
my education in this, or that sect, nor
the authoritie of any eminent man,
nor the fashion of my country in vse
of religion established by estate: but
such grounds as only God can giue,
giue mee the securitie of conscience
which now I possesse: And therfore I
dare boldly say, that if now I be dece-
aued

aued in matters of faith, not man, nor
Angell, but God himselfe
hath deceaued
mee.

FINIS.

ANTHONY BATT

A Poore Mans Mite

1639

A POORE MANS

MITE.

A letter of a Religious man
of the Order of Saint BENEDICT,
vnto a Sister of his, concerning
the *Rosarie* or P*salter* of our
blessed Ladie,
Commonly called the
B*eades*.

✝
IHS

Printed with license of Superiors.

M. DC. XXXIX.

A Poore Mans *Mite.*

A

Letter of a Religious Man

of the Order of S. BENEDICT
vnto a sister of his concerning
the ROSARIE or
PSALTER
of our blessed LADY,
commonly called the BEADES.

Deare Sister.

I Haue sent you a small token of
my no smal loue, a paire of plaine
Beades, together with the explication thereof. The (a) Prophet Dauid vsed to sing certaine spirituall
Ditties or Songs to his Harpe, with

A 2   which

(a) 1. Reg. 18, 19.

which melodie, hee so appeased the
spirit of furie, wherewith King *Saul*
was possessed, and grieuously tor-
mented: that notwithstanding hee
was so incensed against *Dauid*, that
he would haue slaine him: hee was
faine to forbeare, for the great ease
hee enioyed by his melodie, yea and
wh.lest hee sang in his presence, he
had no power to execute his wicked purpose vpon him, as if he had
enchaunted him by the sweetnesse
thereof, as indeede it seemed to
doe. These Songs are called P*salmes*
of *Psallo* a latine word, which in
english signifieth to sing, because
they were sung to the Harpe, and
the whole number of them, are
called *Dauids* P*salter*. They are re-
gistred amongst the Bookes of Ca-
nonical Scripture, and accounted a
principall part thereof so myste-
rious, that they are appliable and
cor-

correspondent to all the affections
and motions of our minde whatsoeuer. They are spirituall Manna,
(b)hauing the taste of euery good
thing we can desire: In regard whereof a certaine Father affirmeth,
Whatsoeuer is contayned in all the
other Bookes of holy Scripture, by
way of Prophecie, Doctrine, or Example; is comprised in this by way
of spirituall Songs, and praytes of
God, the seuerall Verses whereof
are, as it were, so many iaculatorie
darts cast vp to heauen; and therefore they are altogether vsed in the
Church-Seruice and in the Office of
our blessed Lady, commonly called
the Primmer, and in the Manuall of
Prayers, as a most soueraigne and
sanctified deuotion to please God,
and appease the furie of our ghostly

A 3   enemie

(b) Sapient. 16. verf. 20. Exod. 16. verf.
14 Num. 11. verf. 7.

enemie the Deuill, who l ke another *Saul* seeketh the destruction
of our soules. The number of theses
Psalmes are one hundred and fiftie,
and are called, as I said before, the
Psa ter of Dauid.

To the imitation of this holy
Psalter, the Church hath ordained
another diuine Psalter, called the
Psalter of Iesus, commonly set in the
latter end of the Manuall of Prayers
consisting also of the like number,
that is to say, fifteene Petitions,
with ten Inuocations to each Peti-
tion. And to the same imitation, the
Church hath instituted yet another
Psalter, of our blessed Lady, the glorious Virgin *Mary*, commonly called
the *Rosarie* or *Psalter of our blessed
Lady*, or *the Beades*, consisting of
the like number of *Aue Maries*, and
is diuided into three parts, each
part consisting of fiftie *Aue Maries*,
                                    where-

wherevnto are added fiue *Pater no-ſters*, to wit, one betweene euery ten *Aue Marias*, and a *Creede* at the end.

This Pſalter is nothing inferior vnto the other two: but rather ſo much the more ſoueraigne, by how much more excellent the wordes and myſteries thereof are: The *Pater noſter* for ſanctitie and pithyneſſe no Prayer comparable vnto it, pro-ceeding from the ſacred mouth of *Chriſt*, (a) and inſtituted by him as a generall forme of Prayer.

The *Aue Mary*, indited by the moſt bleſſed *Trinitie*, in heauen, and brought as an Ambaſſage, vnto the earth by the Arch-angell *Gabriel*, (b) for moſt ioyfull tydings of the Re-demption of Mankinde, the bleſſed Virgin *Mary* being ſaluted and ho-nored with the miraculous Mother-

A 4 hood

(a) Matth. 6. verſ. 9. Luc. 1. verſ. 29.

hood of the VVorlds Redeemer.

The Creede contayneth the twelue
principall articles of our Faith,
wherevpon as most certaine and
infallible foundations, our holy
Catholike beliefe (without which,
(a) it is vnpossible to pleafe God)
is built, and erected, and was com-
poſed by the twelue Apoſtles, each
of them making one feuerall Article, which in regard thereof, is called in Latine, S mbo um Apoſtolorum,
that is to fay, The Shot of the Apoſtles,
alluding to an Ordinarie, whereas
euery one of the Commenſals lay
downe their shot or share. And as
this Creed is a geuerall Summe of all
our beliefe: ſo are the Pater noſter,
and Aue Marie, generall formes of
prayer and praiſings of God, which
may be applyed to all the particular
affections and motiōs of our minde,
what-

(a) Epheſ.2.verſ.20.Hebr.11.verſ.5.

whatsoeuer wee desire to obtaine at
the hands of Almightie God, as the
Psalter of *Dauid* may. And as our Sauiour Christ commended the *Pater
noster* vnto vs, saying: *When you pray,
pray thus, Our Father. &c.* So our blessed Lady in her Hymne of *Magnifi-
cat,* commended the *Aue Marie* vnto
vs, saying: For, *behold from henceforth
all generations shall call me blessed:* for
with what words, I pray you, can
wee more properly and pleasingly
to God and Her, call her blessed,
then by the *Aue Marie,* wherewithall the Angell *Gabriel* was sent from
Heauen to salute her so, as aforesaid?

The mysterie of the number of
prayers in this holy *Rosarie* or *Psalter*
is this: In the old Law, (a) before
the comming of Christ, euery Fif-
tieth yeere was a yeere of *Iubile,*
wherein

(a) *Leuit.* 25. *verf.* 10.

wherein there was a generall for-
giuenesse of all debts, crimes, and
grieuances whatsoeuer, and a redu-
cing of all things to their former
qualitie and state: in which all grieuances being redressed, the whole
earth did seeme to reioyce, and clap
her hands, and therefore had the
appellation of the yeere of *Iubile*, or
Iubilation, that is to say, of exceeding
ioy and iubilation: and this was indeed a figure of the most ample remission of sinnes in the new Law;
by the Death and Passion of Christ
Iesus, expressed more plainly by
the descending of the holy Ghost
(the Fountaine of Grace and Remission of sinnes) vpon the Apostles
and Disciples of Christ, Fiftie dayes
after his Death and Resurrection,
vpon the feast of *Pentecost* or *Whit-
sunday*, so called, in regard of the
number of fiftie dayes.

Where-

Wherefore by the number of fiftie *Aues Maries*, whereof the third part of the said *Pfalter* consisteth, is aptly signified remission of sinnes. By the fiue *Pater nosters*, is signified the fiue principall wounds of Christ, which fiue wounds may bee resembled to those Cities of refuge in the old Law, (a) as it were, places of Sanctuarie for all Offenders to flie vnto for refuge against their persecuting Foes, either spirituall or corporall. By the ten *Aue Maries* betweene the *Pater nosters*, is signified the ten Commandements. By the *Creede* is signified the Catholike Faith or Beliefe, out of which there is no saluation, or possibilitie of pleasing God, as aforesaid: So that all this put together signifieth thus much, whē we say this holy *Pfalter.* Wee desire that by the keeping of the ten

{Com-

(a) Deuter.15. verf. 2.

Commandements signified by the ten *Aue Maries*, betweene the *Pater nosters*, We being of the Catholike Faith or Beliefe, signified by the *Creede*, in the vertue of the fiue wounds and death of Christ, signified by the fiue *Pater nosters*, wee may obtaine remission of our sinnes signified by the fiftie *Aue Maries*, the number of remission of sinnes, as aforesaid. Besides this, the Church addeth her Benediction or Sanctification to the Beades whereupon they are said, wherewithall I haue caused yours to bee hallowed, to make them (being otherwise but plaine) more precious vnto you.

That the Church hath such authoritie, you need not doubt, it being the vse in the old Law (a) to blesse or hallow, not onely the Temple and Altars, but also all

                      Vestments

(a) *Num. 7. vers. 1.*

Vestments & Vtensils belonging to
the seruice of God. And Saint Paul
saith (*a*) that Creatures are or may
be sanctified by the Word of God
and Prayer, especially that which is
authorised and appointed by the
Church of God to that end, as this
of the Beades is. Moreouer, if there
be any vertue in wordes (as certainly there is) and if wordes can
enchaunt Serpents, as it appeares
they can, out of the Prophet *Dauid*
(*b*) and many naturall experiences
there are of the same. Then surely
it is piously to be thought, that Almightie God is pleased to bee, as it
were, enchaunted with these most
soueraigne prayers deuoutly rehearsed, & hath caused our blessed
Lady and his Saints to bee so likewise : and no maruaile, though he
make himselfe subiect herevnto,
                B   when

I. *Tim.* 4. *verf.* 5. P*fal.* 57.

when he faid to his feruant *Moyfes*,
(a) *Let me goe that my fury may be an-
grie againft this people* : as if *Moyfes*
had forceably with-holden him.

This *Rofarie* or *Pfalter* of our
bleffed Lady, is adorned with fifteene moft pious and deuout Meditations, to wit, of the fiue *ioyous*, fiue
dolorous, and fiue *glorious* myfteries
of our bleffed Lady, well knowne
to moft Catholikes and vfed accordingly, with fundrie other kindes
of godly and deuout Meditations:
amongft which I lighted of late
vpon certaine moft deuout and an-
cient Meditations in latine, called
Rafarium aureum, the *golden Rofarie*,
which, in my opinion, doth very
well deferue that name. Thefe haue
I tranflated into English meeter, &
fet vnto you to ftirre vp & fweetné
your deuotion fo much the more.

If

Exod. 32. verf. 9.

If you obiect the A*ue* M*ary* , pronounced by the Angell *Gabriel* , is no prayer but only a falutation ? I anfwer, The Church hath made it an expreffe Prayer, by adding vnto the Salutation of the Angell , thefe words: H*oly* M*ary mother of God, pray for vs finners, no*w*, and in the houre of our death,* A*men.* Which thing, fuppofing the doctrine of the Inuocation of Saints to bee true, Shee may lawfully doe , and hath great reafon to doe vnto our bleffed Lady as a generall prayer for all vfes efpeciaily, confidering the Salutation was intentionally faid as a prayer, before: and was more then infinuated for fuch by our Sauiour Chrift vpon the Croffe, faying to our bleffed Lady of Saint Iohn (a) *Woman , behold thy Sonne* : and to him of her, B*ehold thy Mother* : by which wordes he
B 2   com-

(a) Ioan. 19 verf. 26.

commended her myſtically , not onely to Saint *Iohn* , but alſo to all others in him , that are *Iohns* by grace and loue of God , as hee was by name , as a Mother of interceſ- ſion to God for them , and they as children confidently to entreat it at her hands.

If your conceit ſuggeſt vnto you, It is a dishonour to God to pray vn- to his Mother ? anſwer vnto it , No more dishonour, then to deſire one anothers prayers here on earth, which is to the greater honour of God, commanded and commended vnto vs in his ſacred Word. If it vrge , The Saints know not our prayers ? anſwer , They reioyce at the conuerſion of a Sinner: There- fore they know the ſame. If the often repetitiō of the ſame prayers ſeeme vaine ? anſwere , It is full of myſterie and holy meditation, as is

before

before declared; which myſteriouſ-
neſſe, together with the often repetition, doe maruailouſly incite the
ſoule to feruour and deuotion, if it
bee done with due attention. The
Angels vſe the repetition of *Holy,
holy, holy.* (a) Our Sauiour Chriſt,
went three ſeuerall times together
into the Garden and prayed (as the
text ſaith) the ſame Prayer. In the
135. Pſalm. the Prophet *Dauid* repea-
teth in euery verſe, *for his mercy en-
dureth for euer.* If one may vſe often
repetitiõ of one thing in the prayſe
of God, Why not in prayer? This
being ſo, this holy *Pſalter* of the
Beades cannot be but a moſt acceptable ſeruice and deuotion to God,
and to our bleſſed Ladie the glorious Virgin *Marie* the Mother of
of God, and to all the Court of
Heauen. And to our enemie the

B 3   Deuill

(a) *Matth.26.verſ.44.*

Deuill a great confufion, chafing him out of our hearts, or at leaft reprefling and much appeafing his deadly affaults and temptations á-gainft vs, as that P*falter* of D*auid* did, as aforefaid, which was in-deed, a liuely figure of this.

Before euery *Meditation following fay the firft part of the* Aue Marie *till you come to* Iefus: Then *fay the* Medi-tation *in verfe : then the other part of the* Aue *Marie in order as it lyeth.*

The golden Rosarie of the most glorious *Virgin* MARY.

Pater noster, Aue Maria, &c.

IESVS.

1 Mary of Virgins all most pure
   Receiue this golden Ro-
      sarie,
Deckt with the life of thy sweet
   Sonne
Vnder a briefe compendiarie.
   IESVS.
2 Whom thou, a Virgin voyd of
   sinne,   B 4   Con-

Conceiuedst of the holy Ghost,

When *Gabriels* newes thou did'st
   beleeue.

  Gayning thereby what *Eue* had
    lost.

IESVS.

3. Of whom thou being great with
    Childe,

  Vnto *Elizabeth* did'st hie,

And *Iohn* the Baptist in her wombe
  Did'st with thy presence sanctifie.

IESVS.

4. Whom in the Citie *Bethleem*
    Thou did'st bring forth with
     heauenly ioy,

Free from those paynes which e-
  uermore

  Womē in Chil birth doe annoy.

IESVS.

5. Whom newly in a Stable borne
  Thou did'st forth with as God.
    adore;

  And with thy Virgins milke distst
    feede,   **A**

A thing most strange, ne're heard
before.

IESVS.

6. Whom thou didst wrapp in sily
   clowts,
   And with brute beasts laid in a
   Manger;
And didst him serue in what thou
   couldst,
   To keepe his tender Corps from
   danger.

IESVS.

7. Whom troopes of Angels, with
   great ioy
   And heauenly melodie did prayse;
Proclayming glorie vnto God,
   And peace to Men on earth al-
   wayes.

IESVS.

8 Who being chiefe of Shepherds
   all,
   The Shepherds of the field first
   found:

And

And finding, worshipt as their Lord
  Though lying poorely on the
   ground.

     IESVS.

9. Who did vouchsafe like sinfull
    man,
  To take the marke of Circumci-
   sion:
And eke the Name of Iesus sweet,
  Our sinfull soules Physition.

     IESVS.

10. To whom three Kings did come
    with gifts
  Of Gold, and Myrrhe, and Fran-
   kincense,
Directed by a blazing starre,
  And him ador'd with reuerence.
    Pater noster, Aue Maria; &c.

     IESVS.

1. Who being fortie dayes of age,
  Thou in the Temple didst present
According vnto Moyses Law,
  Making thy selfe obedient.

       IE-

IESVS.

2. Whom flying *Herodes* perfecution,
　To *Egypt* thou by night didſt
　　carry:
And after comming backe from
　thence,
　In *Nazareth* with him didſt tarry.

IESVS.

3. Whom in the Temple thou didſt
　loſe
　With many a teare and wofull
　hart,
But miſſing him, didſt ſeeke him
　out.
And finding him, didſt glad de-
　part.

IESVS.

4. Whom with the labour of thy
　hands,
　In all his wāts thou didſt ſuſtaine:
And though thy meanes were very
　poore,
　Yet didſt thou neuer once com-
　plaine.　　　　　　　　IE-

IESVS.

5. Whom Iohn in Iordane did baptize
   And pointing to him , thus did
   say:
Behold,the Lambe of God one hie,
   That takes the sinne of Mã away.
IESVS.

6. Whom Sathan in great subtilitie
   Did tempt with sundrie sorts of
   sinne,
To trie where he was God or Man,
   But no way could preuaile
   therein.
IESVS.

7. Who at thy motion did vouchsafe
   To chãge pure Water into Wine,
Confirming his Disciples faith
   By that strange miracle diuine.
IESVS.

8. Who freed such as were possest
   With wicked spirits in bodie or
   minde,
Curing the sicke and lame also,
                              And

And giuing fight vnto the blinde.
IESVS.
9. Who rayfed *Lazarus* frō the graue.
Reftor'd to life the Widdowes
fonne;
Brought home againe the prodigall
Childe
That fuch a defperate race had
runne.
IESVS.
10. Who oft with Sinners did con-
uerfe,
And oft with fuch did take repaft,
And them vnto repentáce brovght,
Forgiuing all their finnes at laft.
Pater nofter , *Aue Maria*, *&c.*
IESVS.
1. Whofe feete the finner *Magdalen*
Did wash with teares of loue and
griefe,
And forrowing deeply for her
finnes,
Obtayned pardon and reliefe.
C   IESVS

IESVS.

2. Who on the holy Moūt of *Thabor*
Caused his bodie so to shine,
That blessed *Peter*, *Iames*, and *Iohn*,
Did see his Majestie diuine.
IESVS.

3. Whom store of people with ap-
plause
With boughes of palme strewing
his way,
Did bring into *Ierusalem*,
But him forsooke that very day.
IESVS.

2. Who, e're he eate the Pascall
Lambe,
Washed his twelue Disciples feet,
Then fed them with his Flesh and
Blond
In Sacrament of loue most sweet.
IESVS.

5. Who in the Garden prostrate
prayde
With sweat of water mixt with
blood, For

For feare of death, yet glad to die,
  If to his Father it feem'd good.
        IESVS.

6. Whom vile and moſt malicious
    Knaues
  Did take, and eke with cordes did
    tie,
And brought him captiue to the
    Iudge.
  Who then was *Cayphas* Bishop hie.
        IESVS.

7. Whoſe comely face (O haynous
    crime)
  With filthy ſpittle they berayde,
And with their firſts full many a
    blowe
  Moſt cruelly thereon they layde.
        IESVS.

8. Whom they to *Pilate* did preſent
  To be condemn'd and iudg'd to
    dye,
Bringing falſe witneſſe to that end,
  Who did accuſe him wrongfully.
      C 2   IE-

IESVS.

9. Whom Pilate vnto Herode sent,
    To dee with him what he best
        deem'd,
Who for his silence sent him backe,
    Clad like a Foole and so esteem'd.
            IESVS.
10. Whose tender Flesh with whips
        they tore:
    Whose sacred Head they crown'd
        with thorne,
In purple garments like a King,
    And so saluted him in scorne.
        Pater noster, Aue Maria, &c.
            IESVS.
1. Whom wounded sore with cruell
        stripes,
    The Souldiers lewdly did deride,
And eke the Iewes with opē mouth
    Did crie to haue him crucifide.
            IESVS.
2. Whom as a Malefactor then,
    Pilate condemned vnto death,
Bearing his Crosse vpon his backe,

Till he was spent & out of breath.
IESVS.

3. Whom on the Mount of *Caluarie*
They stripped naked to the skin;
And setting vp the Crosse an end,
   Did naile him hands and feet
   therein.
IESVS.

4. Who for his Persecutors prayde
Vnto his heauenly Father deare,
And stretched on the bloudie
   Crosse,
His paynes most patiétly did beare.
IESVS.

5. Who vnto the repentant Thiefe,
Of all his sinnes full pardon gaue,
With promise of eternall blisse,
   which he there hanging by did
   craue.
IESVS.

6. Who vnto his Disciple Iohn
Thee for his Mother did comend,
And him to thee as a deare Sonne
          C 3   In

In mutuall loue for to depend.
IESVS.

7. Who when he seemed to com-
          plaine.

His Father had him quite for-
          sooke,
His Foes blasphemed him the more
And no compassion on him tooke.
          IESVS.

8. Who when he cryed out, I *thirst*,
His forces being almost spent,
They gaue him galle and vinegre,
     That so they might him more
          torment.
          IESVS.

9. Who by his Passion finishing
     The prophecies of holy Writ,
Discharg'd the debt of *Adams* sinne,
     Paying his precious bloud for it.
          IESVS.

10. Who then into his Fathers hads
     His sacred Spirit did commend,
Crying alowd with Voyce most
          shrill,   And

And so his blessed Life did end.
Pater noster, Aue Maria. &c.

IESVS.

1. Whose side à Souldier with his
   speare
   Pearc'd, hanging dead vpon the
   Rood,
   And therewithall there gushed out
   A streame of water mixt with
   blood.

IESVS.

2. Who being slaine vpon the Crosse
   His liuelesse Corps did rest in
   peace:
   His Soule went downe to *Limbo*
   lake,
   And did those captiue soules re-
   lease.

IESVS.

3. Whose sacred Body from the
   Crosse
   Ioseph and *Nicodemus* tooke,
   And buried it in noble sort,

                        When

When all men else had it forfooke.

IESVS.

4. Who by his onely power diuine
Did rife againe, being three dayes
dead:
And thee, and his Difciples all,
With his appearance comforted.

IESVS.

5. Who, after fortie dayes were paſt
Afcended into heauen hie,
And at his Fathers right hand ſits,
To raigne with him eternally.

IESVS

6. Who fent from thence the holy
Ghoft
Vpon the feaſt of *Whitſontide,*
Which, his Difciples being weake,
Inflam'de with loue and fortifi'de.

IESVS.

7. Who thee vnto his heauenly
Throne,
Whé thou on earth thy time hadſt
beene,

Aſſump-

Assumpted both in Body and Soule,
 To raigne with him as heauens
    Queene.

IESVS.

8. Who at the latter Day shall come
 And sit as Iudge vpon his Throne,
With rigour and seueritie
 Iudging the deeds of euery one.

IESVS.

9. Who to the bad eternall paynes,
 And to the good eternall blisse,
Will iustly iudge without respect
 Of any person that or this,

IESVS.

10. Who grant, that they which doe
    recite
 This *Golder Rosarie* of thine,
May see th: face of Him and Thee,
 In heauély blisse for aye to shine.

Credo in Deum Patrem, &c.

Ano-

AnotherLetter to his Sister, concerning the Office of our blessed LADY.

commonly called the PRIMMER.

IT is said in the Gospell, that wee must pray alwayes: and Saint Paul exhorteth vs to pray without inter-mission. The meaning of which wordes is not, that wee should doe nothing else but pray , for that wee cannot, nor ought not to doe. The meaning therefore of these places of holy Scripture , is , that wee should pray at certaine set times,
without

(a)Luc .1.v.1.(b)1.Thes.5.vers.17.

without omission or intermission.
Such times did the Prophet *David*
set to himselfe, as appeareth by his
owne wordes: *In the euening and mor-*
ning or at *mid-day*, *Will I declare* or
set forth *thy prayse*: and, P*sal*. 118.*v*.
164.hee saith,hee did the like seuen
times a day.

Our holy Mother the Church,
hath ordayned for Religious and
Ecclesiasticall persons,a certaine set
Office or Seruice to bee said to God,
in euery houre of the day and night
that so they may, seeme to pray alwayes or without intermission, as
aforesaid. But because it were hard
and ouer burdensome to pray euery naturall houre of the day and
night, which are in number twentie foure,Shee hath put three naturall houres into one houre , calling
it a Canonicall or Ecclesiasticall
houre,

(*a*) P*sal*.54.*vers*.18.

houre , and of these there are but
eight in a day and night. For euery
of which eight houres Shee hath
ordayned a seuerall Seruice or Office of prayer and prayssing of God At
mid-night Shee hath ordained that
to bee said,   which we call the Matins : At three a clocke after mid-
night , the Laudes : At sixe a clocke
in the moning, the Prime : At nine a
clocke , the Third : At twelue, the
Ninth: At six, the Euen-song, At nine,
the Compline, so that by this meanes
they seeme to pray alwayes or without intermission , according to the
exhortation of the holy Scripture,
as aforesaid. Thus doe Religious &
Ecclesiasticall persons serue. God
night and day, and doe by their profession binde themselues thereunto,
and this is the publike or common
Seruice and prayer of the whole
Church dispersed thorowout the
                              world,

world, whereof all ſuch as are
members of the Church are partakers, whereſoeuer they are, though
not preſent thereat, but more eſpecially and effectually if they bee
corporally preſent. And that is the
reaſon why deuout people reſort to
Churches vpon Sundayes and Holy
dayes, and many weeke dayes alſo,
not onely to heare Maſſe, but alſo
Matins and Euen-ſong.

Lay people are not bound to anie
ſuch forme of continuall prayer or
ſeruice; but becauſe it is a godly and
deuout exerciſe to imitate Religious and Eccleſiaſticall perſons
herein, and maketh them ſo much
the more effectually partakers
thereof (it being the publike Prayer
or Seruice of the Church) by how
much the more deuoutly they imitate the ſame: Therefore the Church
hath alſo ordained a certaine ſhort,
D but

but verie sweet Office or Seruice
for them to say also, after the same
method or order, called *the Office of
our blessed Lady*, or *the Primmer*, consisting of those seuerall eight houres,
aforesaid. to wit, *Matins, Laudes,
Prime. Third, Sixt, Ninth, Euen-
song, Compline.* Such a booke (deare
sister) I haue sent you, whereby
you may serue our Lord Iesus Christ
and his blessed Mother the glorious Virgin *Mary*, euery our of
the day and night, as aforesaid,
and so purchase the daily and
hourely blessings of God. Not
that I would haue you say these
seuerall Seruices in their proper
seuerall houtes, but to say them
all at two times in the day, in the
Morning and Euening for your
Matins and Euen-song, as the custome is. Or if you cannot conueniently say them at those times;
then

them at such times as you can : And
if you cannot conueniently say the͂
at all, make no scruple to omit the͂,
for none are bou͂d but such as binde
themselues.

Moreouer, besides the saying of
these houres, to the imitation of
Religious persons, that so you may
seeme to pray alwayes or without
intermission, as aforesaid : you may
make another singular benefit by
way of Meditation, according to
the Pictures set downe and prefi-
xed at the beginning of euery
houre, to which end they are
set there.

At your *Matins* you may medi-
tate of the Annunciation or Salutation of our blessed Ladie by the
Archangell *Gabriel*. At *Laudes* of
our blessed Ladies visitation of her
cousin Saint *Elizabeth*. At *Prime*,
of the Natiuitie or birth of Christ.

D 2   At

At *Third* , of the Circumciſion
of Chriſt, and of his bleſſed Name
Ieſus. At *Sixt* , of the Purifica-
tion of our bleſſed Ladie , and
Preſentation of Chriſt in the Temple. At *Ninth* , of the Adoration
of the three Kings and their gifts.
At *Euen-ſong* , of the flight of our
bleſſed Ladie and Saint Ioſeph into
Egypt with little Ieſus. At *Compline*,
of our bleſſed Ladies glorions Aſ-
ſumption body and ſoule into Heauen. Theſe, with the ſeuerall cir-
cumſtances thereof, are moſt ſweet
Meditations, fit to be vſed euery day , and would be very com-
fortable vnto you, if you knew
them perfectly , and were well in-
ſtructed therein. And in theſe exer-
ciſes you shew your ſelfe, as it
were , one of our bleſſed Ladies
eſpeciall Hand-maides, or Wayting-
women , attending vpon her daily
and

and hourely in this Office or Serui-
ce of hers, for such Shee hath and
must haue, as appeareth in the first
Psalme of the second Nocturne at
Matins, *verf.* 15 16. and 17.
and it is the fourth
Psalme in your
Primmer.

D 3   An-

Another Letter to his Sister, concerning the Order of Saint *Benedict*, together with a little Office of Saint BENEDICT.

According to the houres of the Primmer, as aforesaid.

WHen our blessed Father Saint *Benedict* departed this life, the very same time, two religious men saw him ascend into heauen in a rich Robe, with bright Lamps shining round about him, & a Man of a bright and venerable aspect standing ouer him , who said vnto them , while they were gazing on him: *This is the way Which the beloued of our Lord*, Benedict, *ascendeth into Heauen.*

By this way mystically is vnderstood his religious Rule , or course of life , which he instituted and began, and prescribed vnto his Disciples. In this way , not onely Saint *Benedict* himselfe , but also all his Disciples and Followers haue walked, and doe still walke as in a most readie and beaten way to heauen. In this way haue walked fortie sixe Popes (for so many haue there beene of this holy Order or Rule) Emperors, foure : Empresses, twentie two: Archbishops, one thousand sixe hundred: Kings, fortie: Queens, fiftie one : Children of Kings , one hundred fortie sixe : Abbots being Doctors , fifteene thousand seuen hundred:

hundred: Dukes, Marqueſſes, and
Earles, two hundred fortie fiue: A-
poſtles or Cōuerters of Kingdomes
and Countries, thirtie; whereof our
England was one; Saint *Gregorie* the
Great Pope, and one of the foure
principall Doctors of the Church,
ſending thirtie Religious Monkes
of the Order of Saint *Benedict*, who
conuerted it, and eſtablished Catholike Religion therein, in that
perfection that it was called the
Garden of Chriſtendome, and
Dowrie of our bleſſed Lady, the
moſt glorious Virgin *Mary*. Saint
Gregorie being of the ſame Order
himſelfe, and the glorie, not onely
of his owne Order, but of the vniuerſall Church, and for that cauſe
was ſurnamed the *Great:* and of venerable *Bede* called the Apoſtle of
the English Nation. Of this holy
Order of Saint *Benedict* were alſo
of

of militarie Orders of Knights, for
the defence of the Gospell by the
sword, sixe. Of Religious Orders
twelue principall, besides diuers
other lesser, all branches of the holy
Order of Saint *Benedict*, whereof
there were in the world of Mona-
steries of Men, thirtie thousand: &
of Women one thousand and fiue
hundred; who illuminated & filled
all the westerne Church with learning and vertue: it being the onely
Religious Order that was extant in
the westerne Church, the first sixe
hundred yeeres after their beginning, which was about eleuen or
twelue hundred yeeres agoe.

Vnto this Religious Order, the
Dominicans, Francijcans, and *Iesuites,*
three famous Orders of Religion,
are in some part to attribute their
beginnings. Saint *Dominicke* was
giuen to his barren mother, by the
prayers

prayers of Saint *Dominick* Abbot of the Order of Saint *Benedict* , whose name for that cause his Parents imposed vpon him. Saint *Francis* conceiued the first proiect of his religious course, in a Monasterie of the Order of Saint *Benedict*. Saint *Ignatius* (for so he is now newly canonized) receiued the first sparkes of his religious spirit, in a famous Monasterie of Saint *Benedict* in *Spaine*, called *Monteseratta*. Of this Order there were of canonized or approued Saints, *Fiftie fiue thousand fiue hundred and ten,* in the time of Pope *Iohn* the two and twentieth, which was lõg agoe, besides infinite others holy Men and reputed Saints. And we haue had fiue or sixe glorious Martyrs in these our dayes of our small number here in England, Father *Roberts* , one of the first that were sent hither in Mission , being one:

one: (fo happily did they begin) neither did any one hitherto (thankes
bee to God) fall or mifcarry, fo happily haue they gone forwards.

The glorie of the children is to bee
attributed, a great part of it, to the
Parents The branches, buds, blof-
foms and fruit of a Tree vnto the
Roote. Of all thefe aforefaid & infinite others, our moft blefed Patrone Saint Benedict is the Father,
the Founder, the Roote. All thefe
went the way of blefed Saint Benedict, & fo doe likewife all thofe who
ioyne themfelues vnto him in this
holy Fraternitie or Societie of his,
ordayned for lay people, that are
deuoutly affected vnto the Order,
as I vnderftād you are one. Reioyce
therefore and bee glad in our Lord
Iefus, and in his glorious feruant
Saint Benedict, that you are a blof-
fome or bud of fuch a Tree, that
hath

hath fo replenished Heauen and
Earth with fuch noble Fruit, that
you are a Childe of fuch a Father,
and haue fuch and fo many worthy
Brethren and Sifters in heauen and
earth, thofe in Heauen being readie
to draw you vnto them, by the golden chaines of their interceffion &
merits: and thofe on Earth, to lift
you vp with their charitable and
brotherly affiftace, in what they ca:
thefe on Earth being bound fo to
doe, as long as you are of their fraternitie, & walke with them in the
way that our bleffed Father Saint
Benedict did;and they in Heauen out
of their refpectiue charitie can doe
no leffe.

The

The office of the holy *Father*

S. BENEDICT.

At Matins.

Thou, O Lord, wilt open my lips,
And my mouth shall declare thy
praife.
O God, incline vnto mine ayde:
O Lord make hafte to helpe me.
Glorie bee to the Father, and to
the Sonne, and to the holy
Ghoft:

E   A

As it was in the beginning, is now,
   and euer shall be, world without end. Amen.

A Hymne.

AVrora faire vnmask's her face,
   And smiles vpon the earth, to
   see
Saint Benedicts soule, adorn'ed with
   grace,
Ascend to Heauen so gloriously:
How gracious is he there aboue?
Who here on earth did shine so
   bright:
Whose wonders, stonie hearts did
   moue,
And gaue to all the world, his light.
   Praise, honour, glorie, without
   end,
To thee, O sacred Trinitie:
Which Benedict, thy faithfull frend,
Enioyeth for all Eternitie.

                                    An

An Antheme.

There was a man of venerable life, bleſſed in grace and name, who euen from his Chilhood, bearing a graue minde, and tranſcending his age in vertuous conuerſation, gaue his minde to no voluptuouſneſſe.

Verſ. Pray for vs, O bleſſed Father Benedict.

Reſp. That we may be made worthy of the promiſes of Criſt.

A Prayer.

O God who didſt call the bleſſed Father, and Law maker Saint Benedict, from all worldly tumults, to ſerue thee alone: graunt to all & ſpecially ſuch as ſerue vnder his diſcipline, conſtant perſeuerance in vertue, and perfect victorie vnto

their

the'r end Through Iesus-Christ thy
Sonne, who with thee, liueth and
ra'gneth world without end. *Amen.*

At Prime.

O God incline vnto my ayde,
O Lord make haste to helpe me.
  Glorie be to the Father,&c.

A Hymne.

GReat Conductor in sacred
  Warre,
Who neuer conquer'd wert by
  might:
Defend vs with thy holy prayer,
And strengthen vs, when we doe
  fight.
Protect vs from all sinnes disgrace,
Who mad'st the Black bird to re-
  tire:
Which fluttering came about thy
face,   *To*

To tempt thee with vnchaste desire
Praise, honour, glorie, &c.

An Antheme.

Our powerfull Lord, did so great
a fauour to blessed B. nedict, that
vnder one Sun-beame he did see the
whole world.

Veri. Pray for vs, O blessed Father
Benedict.

Resp. That we may be made worthy, &c.

A Prayer.

MAke vs we beseech thee, O
Lord, to imitate here the la-
bours of the blessed Father Saint
Benedict, that there we may be par-
takers of his glorie, through Iesus-
Christ our Lord, Amen.

A

At the third houre.

O God, incline vnto my ayde:

O Lord make haste to helpe me.

Glorie be to the Father, &c.

A Hymne.

TO free thee from vnchaste desire,

Thy flesh the wounds of thornes
indur'd:

And thus fire quenched was with
fire,

And one woúd with another cur'd

With signe of Crosse a poysoned
Cup,

Thou brak'st in two, with power
Diuine;

Which poysó thou hadst supped vp,

But Death was weaker then lifes
signe.

Praise, honour, glorie, &c.

An

An Antheme.

The man of our Lord, Benedict, was of a pleasant countenance, and adorned with Angelicall gray haires, and so great was the brightnesse that shined about him, that being yet vpon the Earth, he seemed to dwell in Heauen.

Vers. Pray for vs, O blessed Father Benedict.

Resp. That we may bee made worthy of the promise of Christ.

A Prayer.

WE beseech thee, O Lord; that the intercessiō of the blessed Abbot Saint Benedict may so recommend vs, that what by our owne merits wee cānot, by his patronage wee may obtayne, through Christ our Lord. Amen.

At

At the sixt houre.

O God incline vnto my ayde:
O Lord make haste to helpe me.
Glorie be to the Father, &c.

A Hmne.

A Monke there was, when o-
thers pray'd,
Oft pull'd away from seruing God:
Who afterwards became most stay'd
When he was touched with thy
rod.
The Earth their bones did vomit
out.
Who did in thy disfauour die.
But those to thee that were deuout,
Did walke vpon the wathers drie.
Praise, honour, glorie, &c.

An Antheme.

The glorious Confessor of our
Lord, Bénedict, leading an Angelicall life vpon earth, was made a mi-
rour

rour of good workes to the world,
and therefore reioyceth in heauen
without end.

Verf. Pray for vs, O bleſſed Father
Benedict.

Reſp. That we may be made Worthy. &c.

A Prayer.

O God, in whoſe power holy
Saint *Benedict* made the dead
mébers of a childe to reuiue, graunt
we beſeech thee, that for is merits,
wee may by the breath of thy Spirit
bee quickned from the death of
cur Soules : through Chriſt our
Lo d. *Amen.*

At he ninth houre.
O God incline vnto my ayde:
O Lord make haſte to helpe me.
Glorie be to the Father, &c.

A

A Hymne.

THe compasse of the World so
 round
He in a Sunne-beame did discrye;
Nothing on earth so strange was
 found
That was concealed from his eye.
O holy Saint! O heauenly Man!
To whom God did his secrets tell,
Who saw the soule of Saint *German*,
Ascend the Heauens, for aye to
 dwell,
Praise, honour, glorie, &c.

An Antheme.

The man of God, *Benedict*, was replenished with the spirit of all
righteous men: pray hee for all Pro-
fessors of the Catholike Religion.

Vers. Pray for vs, O blessed Father
Benedict,

Resp. That we may be made wor-
hy &c.

A

A Prayer.

GRaunt vs, wee befeech thee O Lord, that with cheerefull minde Wee may daily celebrate the memorie of thy blefled Confeffor *Benedict*, whofe life graced with many miracles did well pleafe thee: through Chrift our Lord. Amen.

At Euen-fong.

O God incline vnto my ayde:

O Lord make hafte to helpe me. Glorie be to the Father, &c.

A Hymne.

HIs fifters foule, from finne moft free,
AndBeautified with heauenly loue:
Flie vp to heauens Throne hee fee,
In likeneffe of a milke white Doue.
O blefled Saints of God belou'd,

Who

Who lye intomb'd both in one
  graue:
One heart you had, while here yee
  mou'd,
One glorie now in Heauen haue,
  Praise, honour, glorie, &c.

An Antheme.

Towards the East appeared a
straight way, reaching from his
Cell, euen vnto Heauen, and a Man
of venerable feature, shining in
brightnesse, standing, thereby, de-
manded wose way that was? which
they, confessing they, did not know;
hee said vnto them: This is the way
by which Benedict, the beloued of
our Lord ascended to Heauen.

Ve ſ. Pray for vs, O blessed Father Benedict.

Reſp. That we may be made worthy, &c.

Prayer.

A Prayer.

WE beseech thee, O almightie God, by the merits and prayers of the most blessed Father Sainct *Benedict*, and of his disciples Saint *Placidus*, and Saint *Maurus*, and of the Virgin his sister Saint *Scholastica*, and of all holy Monkes and Nunnes, which vnder his Banner and conduct fought for thee, that thou wouldest renew in vs thy holy Spirit, by whose inspiratiō wee may make warre against the Flesh, the World, and the Deuill and because the Palme of victorie cannot be atchieued, without laborious battell; giue vs in aduersitie patience, in temptation constancy, in perils Counsell: giue vs the puritie of Chastitie, the desire of Pouertie, the fruit of Obedience, and a

F   firme

firme purpofe to obferue thy Commandements, fo that being ftreng-
ned with thy Confolation, and linked in brotherly Charitie, wee may
ferue thee with one heart, and fo
paffe ouer thefe temporall things,
that being crowned for our victo-
ries: we may deferue at laft in the
cōpagnie of thofe Religious troupes, to attaine vnto thofe eternall
good things: Through Chrift our
Lord. Amen.

A *Compline.*

Conuert vs O Lord our Sauiour,
And auert thy wrath from vs:
O God incline vnto my ayde:
  O Lord make hafte to helpe me.
Glorie be to the Father, &c.

A

A Hymne.

Blessed Patriarch wee thee pray,
And also craue in humble wise:
That vnto Heauen thou shew's the
Way,
Whom thou the earth taught'st to
despise.
Grant we may seeke those ioye a-
boue.
And mend in vs what is amisse:
That liuing here in Christian loue,
We may hereafter liue in blisse.

    Praise, honour, glorie, without
end,
To thee O sacred Trinitie:
Which *Benedict* thy faithfull frend,
Enioyeth for all eternitie,
    Amen.

An Antheme.

Let the whole compagnie of all the faithfull reioyce for the glorie of the bleſſed Abbot Saint *Benedict* let the troupes of Religious perſons chiefly exult , celebrating is memorie vpon earth , for whoſe ſocietie the Saints doe ioy in Heauen.

Verſ. Pray for vs, O bleſſed Father *Benedict.*

Reſp. That we may be made worthy, &c.

A Prayer.

PVrifie, O God, the hearts of all thoſe , who forſaking worldly vanities , thou haſt encouraged to aſpire to the reward of a higher vocation , vnder the diſcipline of
their

their holy. Patriarch and founder
Saint Benedict, and powre thy grace
into them, whereby they may perseuer in thee, and by thy assistance
accomplish what by thy inspiration
they haue promised, that so at-
chieuing the perfectiō, which th y
professe, they may also merit to attaine to the reward, by thee pro-
posed, to such as should perseuer in
thee. Through our Lord Iesus-
Christ, who with thee liueth and
raigneth in vnitie of the holy Ghost
Amen.

A filiall recommendation to the most
blessed Father Saint
Benedict.

O Most glorious Father Saint
Benedict, the Gouernour and
F 3   Leader

Leader of such as professe Monasticall discipline, hope, and solace of all them, that heartily implore thy assistance; I humbly recommend mee to thy holy protection, that for the excellency of thy merits, thou wilt vouchsafe to defend me from all euills hurtfull to my soule: and that out of the aboundance of thy pietie, thou wilt obtayne for mee the gift of compunction and teares, that I may worthily and abundantly bewaile my great wickednesse and offences, whereby I haue oftetimes euen from my child-hood, prouoked to anger my louing and gracious Lord Iesus-Christ; and that I may also worthily praise and reuerence thee: O most precious Oliue, and fruitfull Vine in the house of God: O most solid vessel adorned with all kindes of precious stones, chosen according to Gods

ob-*ne*

owne heart , most sweet and with
innumerable gifts of graces , like
so many glistring Pearles embelli-
zed : thee I beseech , thee I
pray , thee with all the affection
of my heart , with all the de-
sires of my soule I implore , that
thou wilt vouchsafe, to be miudfull
of me wretched sinner with Almightie God , that of his infinite
goodnesse , he will bee pleased to
forgiue mee all my sinnes , and
conserue me in vertues; and that
for no cause or necessitie whatsoeuer, he will suffer mee to depart
from him ; but that together with
thee , O louing Father , hee will
admit mee into the companie of
his Saints, and to that blissefull vi-
sion of himselfe , where together
with thee , and that glorious Armie
of Religious persons , who fought
vnder thy Banner , I may for euer
                              enioy

enioy the presence of my God, and
my Lord Iesus Chrift, who with
the Father, and the holy Ghoft, liueth and raigneth, for
euer and euer.
Ameu.

FINIS.

ANTONIO POSSEVINO

A Treatise
of . . . the Masse
1570

A TREATISE
OF THE HOLY
S A C R I F I C E O F T H E
Altar, called the
M A S S E.

In the which by the word of
God, & testimonies of the Apostles, and Primatiue Church, it
is prooued, that our Sauiour
Iesus Christ did institute the
Masse, and the Apostles did celebrate the same.

Translated out of Italian into
English , by Thomas But-
ler, Doctor of the Ca-
non and Ciuil
Lawes.

LOVANII,
Apud Ioannem Foulerum.
Cum Priuilegio. 1570.

*H*IC Tractatus de Sacrosancto Missæ Sacrificio primùm Italicè conscriptus à D. Antonio Possevino, nûc verò in Anglicã linguam côuersus cum suo Archetypo côcordat, & etiã vtilis & Catholicus est, prout intellexi à viris probatissimis vtriusque linguæ peritis, & potissimùm à D. Nicolao Sädero Theologiæ Professore eruditissimo. Actum Louanij, *14*. Martij, Anno. 1 5 7 0.

Thomas Gozeus à Bellomonte, Sacræ Theologiæ Professor.

To the right Reue-
rend Father in God, and my
finguler good Lord, the
Lord Byshop of S. Aßaph,
helth and perpetual
feluitie.

Vch is the estate
(right honorable
and my finguler
good Lorde) of
the Churche of
Chriſt, and ſhippe of S. Peter in
theſe our daies, that as they,
whiche in ſo troubleſome and
tempeſtuouſe a time of the Catholike faith, ſhew them ſelues,
either willingly to be idle be-
holders, either malitiouſly to be
ſcorners and laughers thereat,
may moſt iuſtly be takén to be
if not altogether impiouſe, yet
ɪot ſo louing and worthy mem-
A ij   bers

bers thereof as they ought, fo they which by al meanes force them felues to repell the mife-ries and afflictions whiche are heaped on it daily, ought to be iudged as mofte woorthy chil-dren of the Churche, and to be had therefore in honour, and eftimation.

For whereas the bonde of nature is fuche, that euery man is thereby (no leffe of confci-ence, then of naturall duetie) driuen, to ferue, honour, and mainteine them, by whom cor-porally he hadde his firfte be-ginning (conformablye vnto that the Scripture faith: *Honora Patrem & Matrem tuam*, Ho-nour thy Father and Mother) howe muche more maie the bande of reafon and Chriftian Religion enforce vs to geue al reuerence, honour, and fer-uice

uice to that Mother and thofe
Parentes, which doe fpiritually
geue vs our creation, making
vs not of flefsh, to be prone to
finne, neither of earth to be fub-
ject to death, but of the foule
and fpirite to be inheritours of
heauen, and feloweheyres and Galat. 4
brothers of Chrifte. For it is
the Church of God (faith S. Au-
guftine) whiche being a Mother and a Virgin, both chafte
in body and yet fruitful in bearing children, doth moft fweet-
ly nurfe, and bring vs vppe, endeuouring to make vs as worthy and acceptable children to
God the Father.

Now emongeft many other
great iniuries, which in thefe
daies are offered vnto Chriftes
Church, in my iudgement there
is no greater, then to fay, that
fhee being the Spoufe and my-
ftical bodie of Chrift, hath yet

no outward Sacrifice wherwith
fhe may proteſt outwardly the
honor and ſeruice that fhe oweth vnto God her Maker and
Redemer. For as ſhee confiſteth
not of ſoule onelẏ, but alſo of
body: ſo muſt her Sacrifice be
ſuch, that her body alſo, and not
onely her ſoule, may concurre
to the celebrating thereof, and
ſo ſhal ſhee fulfil the cõmaun-
dement of God perfitly, who
ſaid not onely, thou ſhalt loue
God with al thy heart, al thy
ſoule, and al thy minde: but alſo
with al thy ſtrength and power.
So we ſee our Lorde and Sauiour Chriſt, to haue honoured
his Father, not onely with inward, but alſo with outward Sacrifice made as wel vpon the
Croſſe to redeme vs, as alſo in
his laſt Supper, to the ende we
might in a Figuratiue Propitiatorie Sacrifice, remẽber and be
thankeful

thankful for that true Propitiatorie Sacrifice, which he made
vpon the Altar of his Crosse.

But verely to take away from
the Church al outward Sacrifice, that is none other thing,
then to make her case worse, thā
the case of any other Congregation euer was since the worlde
beganne. In so much that the
Prophetes Azarias, Osee, Ioel,
and Daniel, do reckon it for a
notable plague of the Iewes, to
be at any time depriued of their
publike and external Sacrifices.
Azarias said vnto King Asa after
this forte : If ye feeke the Lord,
ye shal finde him : if ye forsake
him, he wil forsake you. And
many daies shal passe ouer in
Israel without a true God, without a Priest, a Preacher, and a
Lawe. Marke, that where no
Priest is, there is no God : bycause there is no publike pro-
A iiij   fession

2. Para-
lipom. 15

fession of Gods honour, and in a Congregation, that, which is not professed, is accompted not to be at al.

Osee.3. Osee writeth thus: The Children of Israel shal sit many daies without a King, and without a Prince (that is, saith S. Hierom in his Comentaries vpō the same place, without a chief Priest) and without a Sacrifice, and Ioel.1. without an Aultar. Ioel exhorteth the Priest to weepe and lament, *quoniā interijt de domo Dei Sacrificium & libatio,* Bicause Sacrifice and Drinkofferings are lost from the house of God. SyDaniel.3drach, Mysach, and Abdenago lament hereof vnto God himselfe in this wise: There is not (say they) at this tyme a Prince, and Captaine, and Prophet: neither is there a whole Burntoffering, nor a Sacrifice, nor an Oblation, nor an Incense, nor a place

place of Firſtfruits before thee, that we might obteinthy mercy.

Laſt of al, Daniel forſpeaking of the time of Antichriſt, ſaith, that the armes ſpringing from Antiochus (who was the figure of Antichriſt, as S. Hierom there declareth) ſhal take away the continual Sacrifice. The figuratiue continual Sacrifice was mainteined in the Temple of Ieruſalem with the fire of the Altar, which neuer went out. But the true continual Sacrifice is none other beſide Ieſus Chriſt hymſelfe, who continually appeareth before the countenance of God, and maketh interceſſion for vs. And to the end the Chriſtian Churche might wel appeare to be one bodie with Chriſt: he hath left vs alſo the ſelfe ſame Sacrifice of his owne bodie, whiche he ceaſeth not to offer both in heauen euery mo-

Daniel. 9.& 11.

Heb. 9.

Luc. 22

A v ment,

ment, and in earth by certaine courses of time.

The which blessed Sacrifice hath ben at al times beleued in Christes Churche, vntill the Archeheretike of our age Frier Martin Luther, being perswaded against it with a disputation and conference had with the Diuel, wrote against the Masse, as the same Luther himself confesseth in his Booke *De Missa priuata*: as it appeareth in the seuenth Tome of his woorkes printed at Witteberge by Thomas Klugge in the yeare of our Lord 1557. Fol. 228. Wherein Luther setteth foorth in printed books to the open view of the worlde, the whole disputation and coference betwene the Diuel and him on a night as he lay waking in his bedde, about the same Sacrifice of the Masse. And although the said Frier Luther

was

was perſwaded by thoſe ſubtil
argumēts of ihe Diuel, to write
and preach againſt the bleſſed
Maſſe:yet I truſt the goodChri-
ans wil not be ſo lightly ſedu-
ced, as to geue eare to Luther,
or his Maiſter the Diuel,or any
of both their ſcholers,as Muſcu
lus,Caluin,Peter Martyr,Beza,
Iewel, Latimer, Bale, Horne,
and others of their ſect,and new
deuiſed Parlamente Religion:
but wil folow theCatholike and
vniuerſal belief of al Chriſtiás,
what ſo euer arguments the Diuel, or Luther his Scholer, or
any of their followers ſhal ſuggeſt to the contrary. And I deſire the gentle Reader to reade
attentiuely this booke, which
treateth very learnedly and pi-
thily of this bleſſed Sacrifice.

The which booke being writen in Italian by the excellent
Clerke Antonius Poſſeuinus,
                               the

the fame feeming vnto my fmall
iudgement (as wel for the wor-
thineffe of the matter, which is
the moft Diuine Myfterie, and
higheft treafure that Chrift left
vnto his Churche) as alfo for
the perfpicuitie and briefeneffe
of the difcourfe , and deapneffe
of learning and iudgemente)to
be a thing worthy of fight and
memorie: I toke on me to tranf-
late the fame into Englifh.

Wherein although I minded
nothing leffe, then to fuffer it to
come to light or fight of others,
but onely to doe it for a priuate exercife of myne owne:
yet fithens being enforced by
the earneft perfwafiós of fome,
whofe iudgement for their learning and grauitie, I could neither miftrufte, nor well denie
their requeft: I was at the légth
cótent to yeld, and fuffer myfelf
to be ruled therein. And fo being

ing conſtreined to publish and
ſet forth the ſame : I ſaw no man
to whom I was more bounden
to geue it (as a ſmal and ſimple
preſent) then vnto your good
Lordſhip , not that I iudged ſo
baſe and ſmal a thing worthy of
ſo high and beneficial a Patrone
as your Lordſhip is vnto mee,
but that by offering this, which
nowe onely I haue , I mought
(with the poore widow of the
Goſpell) ſhew rather my want
of poſsibility, in not hauing pre-
ſently ſo woorthy a thing as I
would offer, then lacke of good
wil in not offering that I could.

And thus humbly reque-
ſting almighty God (who of the
bowghes and branches hat are
broken of, *Potens eſt* (ſaith the
Apoſtle) *& iterum illas inſerere,*
is able to graffe them on the
ſtocke a newe , and ſo to make
them growe a freſh, requeſting
        him,

Luc.21.

him, I fay, to conuert the harts
of them which, as vngratefull
children, want not to contemne
and oppugne their onely and
true Mother the Church, and fo
to bring vs al to be of one ac-
corde, and one faith, *vt fimus
vnanimes in Domo* : I wifsh vnto
your Lordship helth and pro-
fperitie in this world, and in the
world to come felicitie and life
euerlafting.   At Rome the firft
of Ianuarie. 1570.

> *Your Lordfhips moſt*
> *bounden oratour,*
>   *Thomas Butler.*

He benefite & treasure was so great & singular, which our Sauiour (for an euerlasting pledge, and token, of his tender loue & zeale towardes vs) left vs, in that he did institute the blessed Sacrament, and Diuine Oblation of the Alter: that the Diuel (hauing neuer before found any thing, whereby his Idols and Temples were more destroyed & tourned into asshes, then through it) ceased not to vse al the force, industrie, and malice he might, so to obscure the veritie of so worthy & heauenly institution, that the order of Priesthod (without ỹ which our Law is no Lawe) being thereby

thereby once violate and broken, both the memory of the Passion of Christ should be extinct and troden out, and we also depriued of that liuely meate & sustenaunce, whereby we are made partakers of the celestiall fruite of the Crosse, and become truely knitte, and vnited with God. Thus he, as a most subtil serpent, although at other times he had vnder a coulour and pretence of goodnesse, afflicted the Churche of Christe by diuerse and sundry meanes and pollicies: yet then did he especially shew and discouer to the world, that principally he bent al his might, malice and power, to subuert and deface our most blessed Sacrifice of the Altar, by stirring vp as especial instruments to such a purpose, at one tyme Iulian the Apostata, at an other the Gnosticans, at an other the Arri-

Chrysost in vitalu uentij. & Max. Basilius. Ep. 70. & 72.

Naziaï. de Arr. & seipso & adHero. de exil. reuoc.

To the Reader.

Arrians, the Manichees, the Donatistes, and suche like Heretiques of those times, pronoking and arming them with infidelitie, malice, and impudencie, to procure and worke the ruine of suche things, as were made holy, and consecrate of God, and aboue al to subuerte the Aultars of Christes Churche, from the which that holy Oblation (saith S. Augustine) is dispensed, wherby the sentence, that once passed against vs for our sinnes, was now made void & cancelled. wherein notwithstanding for as muche as this our malitiouse and wicked enemie, knew him selfe not to be of so great force, that he was able to enkendle this so extrauagant and raging fier, vnlesse that man had first transgressed the Lawes and Commaundementes of God, he endeuoured

(to

Optat. in lib 6. ad Parmen.

Leo.1.
epist.75.
Aug.li.9
Confeſſ.

Matth. 4

(to the entent he might thereby
iuſtly ſpoile and depriue man of
the grace he had receiued) to in-
duce him firſt into ſuch a curio-
ſitie, that either generally all
might, with their vncleane and
polluted lippes, taſte of the diuine Scripture (therby to poy-
ſon that ſincere roote of faith,
which of y̆ eternal Father was
planted in our hearts) either, if
that his deſigne tooke not ſuc-
ceſſe accordingly, yet at leaſt to
ſeduce and withdraw ſo much
Chriſtianitie from y̆ right way
of good workes, that after he
might, at his pleaſure, eaſily
ſpoile and robbe them of al the
light, faith, grace, and conſtan-
cie they had. Thus did he theſe
two plagues and calamities
from the beginning of y̆ world
(as it were two moſt peſtilent
and pernictouſe poyſons) ſow,
& diſperſe throughout y̆ whole.
But in this our time eſpecially
hath

hath he planted thereof such a-
bundant variety, and geuen so
great copy of the same, that thei
haue produced already in many
Prouincies, & diuers Nations
such fruites thereof, as haue
made bitter and vnsauery the
whole delectable and pleasaunt
sweetenesse of the Catholike and
Christian vnitie. whereof such
effect hath ensewed, y̆ although
there be many, whose faith hath
not yet ben altered with new=
fangled and peruerse opinions:
yet in them is also sene for the
most part, such a profound and
dead slepe, about either the re=
teining, or desire to recouer the
grace purchased to vs by the
pretiouse blood of Christ, that
they seeme almost vnmindeful
and carelesse of so inestimable a
treasure.

Now in others how lamen=
table is it, such an instability of
belief, such ficklenes and leuity

of

of mind to be in them, that they (being puft vp with the winde of pride & arrogancie) are with euery little blaft of doctrine (be it blowen out of the mouth of neuer so rude, blafphemioufe, & ignorant idiot) turnd & toft into a thoufand changes & rechanges of religion. What fhal I fai of y̆ reft of mē, in whom remaineth fuch a hardnes & blindnes of hart, y̆ the worfe exāple one geueth of himfelf, & the more vnfkilful & void of al knowledge he be in the fecrete & high Myfteries of God (in y̆ inueftigatiō wherof S. Paul fighing cōfeffed, that he could not penetrate fo high as to know them) the more arrogātly wil he prefume to iudge of an other mans ftate & life, to interprete & teache the diuine Scriptures, & to profeffe (as S. Ierome faith) firft to be a perfect Maifter, before he hath learned to be a Scholer. By this

Ad Paulinum.

this meanes is ẙ pure & bright
word of God (but what speake
I of the word?) by this meanes
is Christ him self, and his very
flesh & bloud denied, by this is
the omnipotēcie & loue of God
neglected, and the very Altar of
Christ subuerted, which s. Paul
teacheth vs to be ẙ only remedy   1.Cor.10
to auoid Idolatrie, and finally
(which cānot be repeted wout
teares) by this is ẙ most holie
& diuine Sacrifice of the Altar,
with blasphemous & impious
words, called abominatiō, & we
that are Catholikes, are named
Idolaters, no otherwise then ẙ
Christians were so called of the
Manichees and Pagans in the
time of S. Austine, bicause they
did in the holy Oblation of the
Altar, adore Iesus Christ. Nei-
ther doth ẙ maligne wickednes   Aug.lib.
of the Diuel, cease or acquiet it   20. in
self herein, but it excourseth far-   Faust.
ther forth, causing that in place   ep.13.

of

of thofe fhining & bright lights
of the Primitiue Church, which
being kendled of the fier of the
holy Ghoſt) did ſet foorth and
manifeſt vnto vs , the Catho=
like and true Chriſtian faith , &
in ſteede of thoſe holy and blef=
ſed Fathers, who (like ſtedfaſt
& ſure pillers, left vs the whole
frame of Chriſtes Church vpō
moſt aſſured, good and certaine
foundation) cauſing, I ſay, that
in place of theſe, are onely read
ſuch impious writings, and ab=
hominable bokes , ſo ſtuft with
lies , and blaſphemies, ſo ful of
authorities malitiouſly & falſely
alleaged, ſo coloured with wic=
ked and infamous titles of he=
retical nouelties , that a Chri=
ſtian eie can not without teares
abide to beholde them. wheras
therefore the impugnation of
the true faith and Catholique
doctrine of Chriſt are ſuch, they
being ſo perilouſe as they are,
and

and so great: it hath pleased the
holy Ghost so to worke with
many, that for the loue & zeale
they beare to God, they haue
freely & frankly taken on them
the defence and protection of
Gods cause, thereby disclosing
in the same, many points and
mysteries, which otherwise had
ben sufficient to be rather sim=
ply beleeued of the rude and
vulgare people, then curiously
to be sought out, and arrogātly
knowen. wherof vnto me also
hath ben ministred occasiō (mo=
ued partly by the counsel & re=
quest of others) to suffer this
my briefe Treatise to come to
light. where briefly is compre=
hended a short collectiō of such
testimonies and reasons, as do
confirme the veritie of y̒ blessed
Sacrifice of the Altar. For sith
I am in such place & state, that
almost howrely I am forced to
heare a thousand impieties a=
gainst

The Prologue

gainst so miraculouse and Diuine Mysteries, it semed requisite, that by sundry waies eche one should endeuour to oppose against the Diuel some one or other stoppe and staie in the behalf of the truth, that he finding him selfe destitute thereby of so free a scope to wound the harts of Christias, as he would haue, might be forced (in spite of his teeth) to geue due honour to Iesus Christe , and withall to suffer the vniuersal doctrine of the Catholike faith (through y̑ helpe of the holy Ghost) to remaine in his owne proper puritie and brightnesse.

You therefore, which shal reade this present Treatise(for asmuch as y̑ wisedome of God, as the wise man saith, entereth not into vncleane and defiled hartes) must especially eschew and abandon as well the cogitation, as practise of al such doings,

Sap. 12.

ings, whereby the eyes of the Diuine Maiestie may iustly be offended: that by seeing therby the celestial worthinesse, & inestimable frute of thys so vnspeakeable and tremend a Sacrifice, ye may hereafter with a more vehement zeale, & ardent charitie, endeuour to be partakeners of the same: and so honouring with true and intier affectiō, the giftes of the goodnesse of our Lord, ye may (as bounden duety requireth) render all glory and praise to his Diuine Maiestie: To whome be all honour and laude, now and euer. Amen.

A table of the
Chapters.

Chriſt

B ij   How

OF THE MOST
HOLY SACRIFICE
of the Altar, which is called the Masse.

The First Chapter.

WHEREAS we entend to entreate (according to ẏ true sense & meaninge of ẏ holy worde of God) of ẏ veritie and excellencie of the Sacrifice of the Altar (whiche commonly is called the Masse) it semeth to be as wel requisit for the vnderstanding thereof, as also consonant to good methode and order, first to declare and define what thing properly is a Sacrifice. A Sacrifice therefore proprely may be defined, to

B iij   be an

be an acte or operation, by the
which some one thing is conse=
crate & offered vp to God, ther=
by as wel to appeace his wrath
& indignation towardes vs, as
also to geue him due reuerence
and honour in recognising the
supreme dominion of his Di=
uine Maiestie: although we of=
fer him nothing els, but the self
same things which we receaue
of him.

Ambros.
lib.4. de
sacra.c.6.
De ciuit.
Dei.li.10
cap.6.

The end wherfore Sacrifice
is done, is (as S. Augustine
saith) to make vs by a holy and
blessed felowship, to be coupled
& ioyned with God, to whome
that our worke and operation
is referred, as vnto such an end
of perfection and goodnes, by
the which we may vndoubted=
ly become blessed and happy.
The substantial & proper parts
of Sacrifice are, the Consecra=
tion, the Oblation, and the re=
ceauing or eating: to these chief
partes

partes are conſequently alſo re=
quired, both the authoritie to
make it, & alſo the meanes ne=
ceſſary and inſtruments apper=
taining to the ſame: as Prieſt=
hod, Altar, Chalice, and other
the like things, wherof both in
the Olde Scripture generally,
& alſo particularly in the New,
mention is made noleſſe by our
Sauiour himſelf (by ẏ mouths
of his Euangeliſts)then by his
elect veſſel S. Paule, as here=
after we ſhal more at large de=
clare.

  Foure things principally are
to be conſidered in euery Sacri
fice. 1. To whome it is offered
(for it is conuenient onely for
God) 2. By whom it is offe=
red, ẏ is, by a man which is in=
ſtitute in holy Orders of Prieſt=
hod. 3. what thing is offered.
4. And for ẏ ſaluatiõ of whom.
Nowe,ſith then Sacrifice is an
action, which in a moſt excel=
       B iiij   lent

Leuit.
Exod.
Num. &
aliâs.
Matt.26.
Mar.14.
Luc.22.
1.Cor.10.
Heb.vlt.
Augu.de
Trinit.
li.4.c.14.

lent wise is conuenient only to
God, and to men, neither vn=
to Angelles, for as muche as
God onely is a most sufficient
meanes to obteine and geue
vs the graces whiche we de=
maunde of him : it foloweth,
that by all meanes the Sacri=
fice of the Law of the Gospell
ought to be a better Sacrifice,
and in a farre more perfit sort,
then either that was of ỹ Law
of Nature, either of the Lawe
of Moyses.

Heb.7.

This Sacrifice could be no
other (as S. Paule proueth)
then that which was after the
order of Melchisedech, ỹ which
shal no lesse, saith he, continew
euer vnto the end of the world,
and vnto the last comming of
our Lord at the daie of iudge=
ment, then now it doth succede
after that Sacrifice, which was
by the order of Aaron. where=
fore S. Augustine (cōformably
to the

Li 2.cōt.
Fauſt.
c.21.17.

to the faith of all Christianitie)
speaking of this, saith: that we
doe oftentimes sacrifice vnto
God, only after those rites and
ceremonies, with which Christ
in the publishing and manife-
station of his new Testament
commaunded vs to doe: as the
whiche doo apperteine to that
kind of worshipping, which is
calledLatria, that is to say, such De ciuit.
adoration as is due to be geuē Dei. lib.
to God only. And in an other 10.c. 20.
place he writeth: For this cause &Conci.
is he both the Priest, saith he, 2.inPſ.32
that is, the partie whiche doth & 33.
offer vppe, and also the oblati- Ieſ.10.
on and offering it self: the Sa- ſer.150.
cramente whereof he hath or- de temp.
deined to be a daily Sacrifice
of the Church. And againe els
where he addeth, and saith in
these woordes : Christe of his
owne body and bloud hath instituted the Sacrifice after the
order of Melchisedech

              B v   It

Cypr.li.2
epiſt 3.
Aug. de
ciuit.Dei
li.16.c.22
Pſal.109.
ep.59. &
li.1.cōtra
Adu.Leg
& Proph.
cap.19.
Hieron.
ad Mar-
cellam.
Ambro.
lib.4.de
ſacra. &
lib.5.c.1.
Arnob.in
Pſal.109.
Damaſ.
lib.1. de
fide orth.
cap.14.
Origen.
parte 1.in
Leui.24.
hom.13.

It remaineth therefore, that the truth hereof be ſet forth and ſeene more at large , as well by the Figures and Prophesies of the Olde Teſtament,as also by the teſtimonies of many & ſundry places of the New , which by Gods grace we ſhall doe in the Chapters folowing.

The Sacrifice of the Maſſe was figured inthe old Teſtament.
Cap. II·

THe Sacrifice of the Altar (ſaith S . Cyprian, and S . Auſtine , with other writers neare to y Primitiue Churche) was figured by the bread & wine which was offered of Melchiſedech : and by the Shewe bread (as y moſt auncient writer Origen ſheweth) and alſo by one of the two Goats which was let go looſe in the deſert,whereas the other which

which was killed in Sacrifice, was a figure of the bloudy offering of our Sauiour Iesus Chriſt on the Croſſe. Whereof this vnbloudy Sacrifice, of the which we now entreat, taketh al his ſtrēgth. And to be ſhort, as touching ẏ thing conteined in the Sacrament of the Altar (which is Iesus Chriſt) al the Sacrifices of the Old Law (eſpecially that of expiation which was very ſolēne) were figures of this our Sacrifice. As touching ẏ effect, Manna was a figure therof, but as touching al theſe things togeather, a moſte propre & manifeſt figure therof was ẏ Paschal Lambe, as S. Chryſoſtom and S. Ambroſe, maiſter vnto S. Auguſtine, do declare. The Lamb was offred (ſaith S. Ambroſe) & the Calfe was offered: but now is Chriſt offered vp, yea he as a Prieſt, offereth vp himſelfe, to the end

he

Io.6. & Cypr de cœn. Do. Chriſoſt. hom. 82. in Matth. Ambr. li 1.offic.

Li.1.offic

he may pardon vs our sinnes.

Besides this , as the Lambe which was in Sacrifice offred vp, was really eaten : so we (to ꝑ entent ꝑ al may be most perfitly fulfilled of Christ) ought really to feed of his most pretiouse flesh and bodie. And it was very conuenient (saith S.

Li.2.ep.3 Cyprian) ꝑ (if we would drink of Christes bloud) Christ himself should first be pressed and in Isai 63 trodē on ꝑ presse of the Crosse. De ciuit. S. Augustine speaking of the Dei.c.20 Sacrifice of Christes Church, lib.10. cōfirmeth al this, & saith: Sundry & diuers signes of this true Sacrifice, were ꝑ old Sacrifices of ꝑ holy Fathers, figuring & setting forth to our eyes, this one by a great many, as one thing is said by many wordes, to the end it might wout great fastidie, be the better recōmended and more acceptable to vs, and finally he concludeth , that

to

to this true Sacrifice all other
false Sacrifices did yelde and
geue place.

The Sacrifice of the Masse was
prophecied and forespoken
of by the Prophetes.

Cap III.

THe Prophet Dauid saith Psal.71.
Erit firmamétum in ter-
ra in summis montium,
There shall be a firma=
ment in the earth, on the toppe
of the hilles. The Hebraicall
Translation hath: ther shalbe in
earth a wafer or cake of wheat. Proph. 1.
Erit in terra placenta frumenti.
The Chaldaical Translation,
which was before ỹ cõming of
Christ, is: ther shalbe, Corban,
ỹ is to say, a Sacrifice of wheat
in the earth, vpõ the top of the
hilles of the Church, ỹ is, ouer
the head of the Priestes & Pre=
lates of the Church,

The

The very Hebrew Doctours themselues, especially the Rabbine Kymhi, and the Rabbine Salomone do affirme, that this Psalme is vnderstāded of Messias, and further they adde, that the Sacrifice of Christ ought to be made with a wafer or cake of wheat. Likewise the Rabbine Iohai proueth, that the Sacrifice of bread & wine should neuer cease, as wel by this place, as also by that which is in the Booke of the Iudges, writen in these wordes: Can I abandone my wine, whiche doeth make ioyful & merie both God and Man? And therefore the said Rabbine addeth: Admitte that wine doth make men ioyful, yet how can we say, that it maketh also God ioyful? And he answereth to himself, saying: This shall be in the Sacrifice which shal be made of the same wine.

Roffen. de Sacer-dotio cō greſſu 2. cōtraLu-ther. art. 45.

Iudic 9. Profetia. 2.

Also

Also the Rabbine Pinhas, the sonne of Jair, saith: At the time of Messias all Sacrifices shal cease, but that of bread and wine shall neuer cease, as it is said in Genesis, the fourtenth Chapter: Melchisedech ꝩ King of Salem tooke bread & wine. Melchisedech saith he, that is, the King Messia, bycause he is called Melech, whiche is as much to say, as a King, sith he is the King of al the worlde: & Sadech significth Justice: and he shall send his iustice and his peace vpon the whole worlde. And it foloweth: The King of Salem, that is, of the supreme Hierusalem, tooke bread and wine, which doth inferre, that he wold separate from the ceasing of the Old Sacrifices, the Sacrifice of bread and wine: as it is said in the 109. Psalme: Tu es Sacerdos in æternum, secúdùm ordinem Melchisedech, Psal. 109.

Thou

A Treatise of the

Thou arte a Prieste for euer, after the Order of Melchisedech.

Proph.3.
Roff. cō-
greſſu 2.
de Sacer-
dotio cō-
tra Luth.
art. 45.

The Prophet Dauid then did prophecie and foretell of the Sacrifice of the Altar, in the woordes abouesaid, forasmuch as Melchisedech (as the Rabbine Samuel, alleged by the Rabbine Hadarsan, vppon the declaration of the place of the Genesis saith) gaue vs the Mysteries of Priesthoode, being him selfe one that did sacrifice vnto God, and that did blesse the bread and wine, and was a Prieste vnto the same God most high and Omnipotente.

Gen.14.
ep.3.li 2.

Our Lorde and Sauiour (saith S. Cyprian) doing most perfectly, and fulfilling this selfe same thing, offered vppe bread, and the Chalice mingled with wine: and so he which is the fulnesse and plenitude it selfe it selfe, fulfilleth the truth of the Image that was prefigured. Then (saith S. Augustine) was Abraham blessed of Melchisedech, the whiche was a Priest of the moste high God. where first appeared plainely the selfe same Sacrifice, which nowe is offered vp vnto God, in the whole worlde. And after, in æternum, saith Dauid, bycause this new Sacrifice instituted of our Sauiour Christ the true Priest, should perpetually remaine in the Churche of Christ.

De ciuit. Dei.li.21 cap.17.

Ezechiel the Prophet did also noteise prophecy of this perpetual continuance of it. Dauid my seruant (saith he) is a Prince and Lord ouer them for euer: & I wil make with them a truce and a couenant of peace (that is, Christ whiche is our peace) it shal be an euerlasting truce & couenāt vnto them: & I wil

Aug.in Psal.33. Proph. 4. Cypr. de cœn.D. Perpes est hoc sacrific. Ezech.37

wil found them (that is, I wil
plant and place them on a sted=
fast and sure rocke o2 stone)and
will multiply them (meaning
by regeneration in Baptisme)
and will geue my Sanctifica=
tion in the middest of them fo2
euer. that is , I wil geue them
the very blessed body and flesh
of Ch2ist.

The Seuenty Interp2eto2s
did mo2e plainly expound these
wo2des,saying : And I wil put
my holy things in the middest
of them for euer. Now the P2o
phete vnderstandeth by holie
things, the most blessed body &
bloud of our Sauiour Ch2ist :
as also S. Paule aduertised vs
speaking of the resurrection of
the bodie of our Lo2de Jesus
Ch2ist, and alleaging the P2o=
phet Dauid which saith : I wil
geue you ye holy things of Da=
uid,which are faithful,& there=
vnto addeth, that is els where
w2itten :

Actor.13.
Psal.15.

writen: thou shalt not suffer thy holy to see corruption (that is, thou shalt not permitte that the body ot our Lorde may be corrupted in the graue) and so finally to this ioyneth Ezechiel: And my Tabernacle ſhall be emongeſt them, and I will be vnto them a God, and they ſhal be vnto me a people. In the which place he called the body of Chriſt a Tabernacle, in the which the plenitude and fulnes of the Diuinitie is remaining, and wherein we alſo do enhabit, and are permanent, feeding our ſelues with the moſte pretiouſe Bodie of our Sauiour, which to that ſelf ſame purpoſe ſaid : He that cateth my fleſh, remaineth in me, and I in him. So likewiſe doth S. Paul vnderſtand by the Tabernacle, the bodie of our Lord, declaring the wordes of the Prophet Amos,

Ezech. cap.37.

Ioan.6.

Actor.13.

iij

Heb.9.
Proph.5.
Prou.9.

Li 2.ep.3
& Hier.
in Prou.
cap.9.

Proph.6.
cap.31.

in writing vnto the Hebrews.
Salomon also did no lesse fore=
tel this self same Sacrifice, say=
ing: wisedome hath built her a
house, and hath vnderpropt it
with seuē pillers, shee hath kil=
led her Sacrifices & offerings,
shee hath mingled wine in the
Chalice and prepared ẏ Table.
S. Cyprian expounding this
same place, saith: The holie
Ghost sheweth before a figure
of the Sacrifice of our Lorde,
making mention of the host of
bread and wine, that is sacrifi=
ced, and withall of the Altar, &
of the Apostles. Ieremie like=
wise ẏ Prophet speaking of ẏ
continuance of this Sacrifice,
saith: The holy of ẏ Lord shall
not be rooted vp, nether be de=
stroyed in any time to come fo2
euer. The Prophet had before
spoken at large of ẏ comming
of Christ, & of the things which
by him should in time of grace

be

be either changed oz fulfilled.
S.Paule reciteth the selfe same Heb. 7. 8.
Authoꝛitie, interpꝛeting it of
Chꝛist ẏ new Bishop, who was
to institute a new Sacrifice in
stede of that old of Aaron, and a
new couenant and Testament
vnto a new people (which are
the Chꝛistians) by abꝛogating
& taking away the old Sacrifi=
ces. Foꝛ by saying a new (saith Heb. 7.
S.Paule) he made the foꝛmer
olde, whereby the same being
now cancelled and made olde,
is also become as dead.

    whereas then the Pꝛophet
Ieremie saith: a new couenant
and testament, a Law, & a Cit=
tie, and a people newe, from
whom ẏ Holy of the Loꝛd shal
not be extirpate, he geueth vs
manifestly to vnderstande the
cõtinuance of this perpetuall
Sacrifice, accoꝛding to the oꝛ=
der of Melchisedech, with the
whiche he woulde be adoꝛed.
                          And

Hier.li.6.
in Ier.c.6
Profet.7.
Daniel.
12. Hier.
in Dan &
Hippol.
Martyr.
paraphr.
in Dan.à
Hier.ci-
tat.

And this self same sence doth likewise S. Hierome gather & confirme vpon the same place. Daniel the Prophet saith: Many shal be elected & made pure and white, and many shall be proued as the fier, and ẙ wicked shal do wickedly, but the learned shall vnderstande at what time ẙ continual Sacrifice shal be taken away, and abhomination shall be sette in desolation, a thousand, two hundreth, and ninety daies. This Prophesie shal truely be fulfilled in the time of Antichrist, as our Sauiour sheweth in S. Matthew, and S. John signifieth in the

Apoc.12.

Apocalipse: where also in some parte it answereth (as S. Chrisostome iudgeth) to the destruction of Hierusalem, which yet was but a figure of the last desolation of the Churche, and of ẙ continuall Sacrifice of Christ whiche shall neuer ceace before those

those last daies. Theodosion (which translated the Old Testamente out of the Hebrew tongue, sheweth also, that this Prophesie apperteineth vnto ye time that is neare vnto the resurrection, by translating it in this sorte: Thou Daniel, goe thou and repose, and thou shalt rise againe in thy order, in the end of the daies. In that time therefore, shal vndoubtedly the Church be desolate, although the Diuel hath many hundreth yeares before, now by ye Gnosticans, nowe by the Arrians, now by Iulian the Apostata, & nowe by the Donatistes, and other the like Infidels, assaulted to destroy this moste holy Sacrifice, and the things to it apperteining. Malachias the Prophet saith: From the East to the west greate is my name emong al Nations, and in euery place is sacrificed & offered

vp

Hier. in Dan. 12. Basil. ep. 70. & 72. Gregor. Nazianz ad Hier. de exil. reuoc. Chrysost in vita Iuuentij, & Maximi. Mar Optat. in li. 6. cont. Parmen. Leo 1. ep 75. & Athanas in vita D. Ant. apudHier. Mal. 1. 3. Profet. &.

Martial. disc.

Christi vnus ex 72 ep. ad Burdeg.

Euseb.de Euse.li.1. cap.10 & li.2.c.29.

Hier.in c.1.Mal.

Li.4.c.32 & li.1.c.3

Damas. li.4.c.24

Chrisost. hom.32. in cap.4. Ioan.

vp vnto my name, a pure Oblation: for my name is greate emong the Nations, saith the Lord of hostes.

This Prophete Malachie was the last of the twelue lesser Prophetes of the Olde Testament, who with his Prophecie beganne to denounce vnto vs, the comming of S. Iohn Baptiste, and after speaketh of the Religion of Christ, which was to come at what time shoulde be offered vp a most holy Sacrifice in stede of al the Olde sacrifices, not in one place onely, but in the vniuersall worlde. wherevpon the holie Martyr S. Irenee, the hearer of Polycarpus, Disciple to S. Iohn the Euangelist, saith, that vntil his time, that is, a thousand and foure hundred yeares past, this offering was offered vp vnto God, in all the partes of the worlde, the whiche (saith he) the

the Church hath receiued of the
Apoſtles.

The Figures and Prophecies a-
boue ſaid were fulfilled of our
Lord in the inſtitution of the
Sacrifice of the Altar.

Cap. IIII.

THe Sacrifice of ẙ Maſſe
as touching al ẙ things
whiche ſubſtantially do
appertain to a true Sa-
crifice) was wholy inſtituted of
our Lorde Ieſus Chriſte, the
which (ſaith S. Cyprian) euen
vnto this preſent daie doth cre-
ate, ſanctifie, bleſſe and diſtribute this his moſt true & bleſſed Bodie.   Firſt therefore did
our Lord inſtitute the Conſecration, the which (as he himſelfe teſtifieth, with other holy
and auncient wꝛiters) is done
with a ſolemne benediction of
this ſubſtantiall bꝛeade, and of
C   this

De cœn.
Dom.
Aug. li. 1.
de Trin.
c. 4 to. 3.
Cypr. de
cœn. D.
& lib. 2.
ep 3. de
Conſecr.

this Chalice, the which do help much vnto the life and saluation of the whole man. Next did our Sauiour transmute and change the nature and substāce of breade & wine, into his true body and bloud, by the meruelouse efficacie of his holy word, whiche hath no lesse force and vertue then fier (wherunto it is in the holy Scriptures likened) which chāgeth and transmuteth the wod into his owne nature: neither is it of lesse strength, then the stomake and other inward parts of our bodies, the whiche doe transmute and change bread and wine into our flesh and bloud. The which thing (saith S. Austine) when by the handes of men it is brought to that visible forme and shape, it is not sanctified (that it may be a great Sacrament) but only by the spirit of God inuisibly working in the same:

Psal. 118.

Transubstātiatio.
Aug. li. 3.
de trinit.
cap. 4.

same : syth it is God onely,
which worketh al those things
which are don in the same ope=
ration by corporall motions
(that is to say, by the mutation
of the bodie or substaunce of
bread and wine into the flesh
and bloud of our Sauiour) mo=
uing (addeth S. Augustine)
the inuisible things of the Mi=
nisters, or the mindes of men,
or y̆ powers of secrete spirites,
which are subiect vnto his Di=
uine Maiestie.

This common bread (saith
S. Cyprian) being changed in=
to flesh and bloude, procureth
life & encrease vnto our bodies:
and a litle after addeth : This
bread, which our Sauiour gaue
vnto his Disciples, chāged not
in the externe forme y̆ is, in the
outward apparāce) but in na=
ture, is (by the omnipotencie of
his holie word) made flesh. For
as in the person of Christ, his

Cypr. de
cœn. D.

C ij   huma=

humanitie was seene, but his Diuinitie laie priuie and hidden: so in this visible Sacrament, that is vnder the forme of breade and wine which we see, is vnspeakeably conteined and enfused ý Diuine substāce of Gods Deitie. S. Ambrose herevpon saith: Yf the words of Helias preuailed so muche, ý they were able to make fier to descend from heauen: shall not the word of Christ haue so much force and efficacie, that it may change one substance into an other?

De ijs q̄ initiātur myst.c.9 tom.4.
4.Reg.1.
Gen.1.

Ioan.c.1.

Of al the workes of ý world it is read in ý holy Scripture, that he spake the woorde, and by and by were the thinges done. And in good sooth (saith Cyril) it is no lesse possible to our Lord & Sauiour, to change the substance of bread & wine into his bodie and blond, then it was to him to change water into

Cyril.Hierosol. in 4.cathe. Mystagogica de S. Euchar
Ioan.2.
Matt.26.

into wine: and therefore is it
our bounden duetie, with no
leſſe aſſured and ſtedfaſt faith to
beleue & obey our Lord, which
ſaid to vs: Doe ye this: then
the ſeruaunts of the Architri= Oblatio.
cline obeyed at that tyme the
bleſſed Mother of our Lorde, Dionyſ.
which had tolde them : Do ye lib. Hier.
what ſoeuer he ſhall bid ye do. Eccl.
After this did our Lorde inſti= Luc.22
tute the Oblation, and withal Tom.4.
did offer vp himſelfe in his laſt Hom.2.
Supper vnto his Father, the & in 2.
which doth wel appeare in his ad Tim.
geuing of thankes, and in the &li.3.c.4
eleuation and lifting vp of his de digni
eyes, the which things we (by Sacerd.
the tradition of the Apoſtles) & ho.78.
do alſo obſerue, and by ſaying: in Ioã. &
This is my bodie which is ge- hom.17.
uen for you. epiſt. ad
Heb.10.

That holie Oblation (ſaith Tom.4.
Chryſoſtome) whether Peter hom.2. et
or Paule, or any other Prieſt in 2. ad
doth offer it (of what ſo euer Tim.
C iij   merite

merite he be) is the selfe same,
which Christ himself gaue vnto
his Apostles, & now Priests do
consecrate. And why is this?
Bycause (saith he) men doe not
sacrifice it, but Christ which be=
fore had sacrificed it. Wherupō
saith S. Austine, the Christians
do celebrate the memorie of the
self same Sacrifice with ŷ Ob=
lation & participatiō of ŷ bodie
& bloud of Christ. Farthermore
did our Lord institute ŷ recea=
uing and eating of the same, by
geuing his pretiouse bodie and
blud to be catē of his Disciples
saying: Take and eat, this is my
body, and this is my bloud.

    Thus do we see here all the
substantiall partes of a perfect
Sacrifice: the whiche things
being done of vs (as S. Au=
gustine sheweth) to the ende
we may be vnited truely with
God: we shal be moste assured,
that as our Lord vnited mans
nature

Marginal notes:

Ambros.
de sacra
Virg. Ni-
ceph. Ec-
clesf.hist.
li.1.c.28.
Tom.5.
li.18.c.22
De Ciuit.
Dei.& de
Spi.& lit.
c.11.li.20

Cap.18.
contra
Faust.

nature with is Diuine , by
taking on him our flesh : so we
shalbe ioyned with his Diuini=
tie by receauing this his moste
gloriouse flesh, conformably to
that S. Paule writeth : we are
al one bodie which do partici=
pate of one bread, which is the
flesh of Christ. The bread (saith
our Lorde) which I will geue
ye, is my flesh for the life of the
world. Afterward he gaue au=
thoritie to his Apostles , and
Priests only, to make and cele=
brate this holy Sacrifice , as
being a thing most iust & con=
uenient , y such should in some
special manner be holy & cóse=
crate, as specially shuld handle
things so Diuine & Celestiall.

Besides this , did he com=
maund the very same to con=
tinew for euer, saying: Do this
for the remembrance of mee :
y is, Do this holy actió, which
I haue done , taking breade

Mandu-
catio.
De Ciuit
Dei.li.10
cap.6.
1.Cor.10.
Ioan.6.
Concil.
Nicen.
c.14.
Athanaf.
cap.6.de
mirac.
crucifixi.
Bafil.
De ritu
Sacrificij
& forma
Missæ
celebr.

C iij   and

Dionyſ.
Eccleſ.
Hierar.
c.3 par.3.
Cypr li.2
epiſt 3 &
de cœ.D.
Chryſo.
hom.83.
in c. 26.
Matthe.
Aug.de
Trinit.
li.4.c.14.
& lib.20
cap.25.
contra
Fauſt.
Chryſoſt.
& Baſil.
liturg.
German.
Epiſcop.
Conſtât.
de Hiſt.
Eccleſ.&
myſtica
contem
platione.

and wine, and lifting vp your
eyes, rendring thankes, conſe-
crating and offering my bodie
and bloud to my Father, for ý
remembrance of my death, that
by meanes of ſo great an offering of my ſelf, he may be made
mercifull and propitiatorie to
your ſinnes. Chriſte had not
(ſaieth Germanus an Arche-
biſhop, a very auncient Greke
writer) commaunded his Apoſtles to doe this, vnleſſe he had
alſo geuen them power to doe
it. Do ye (ſaith God in the Old
Teſtament) a Lambe, a Kidde
for your ſinnes : Doe ye two
Turtle Doues, or a Goat: Do
ye ſeuen Muttons and ſeuen
Calues, that is to ſay, offer ye
vp, and ſacrifice ye them. For
ſo in many other places, as
when Elias ſpake with ý Prophetes of Baal, oftentimes he
vſeth this word facere, pro ſa-
crificare, to doe, in ſtede of, to
ſacri-

ſacrifice. So did S. Hierome tranſlate, thou shalt offer, that which in the Pſalme is written, thou shalt do to thy ſelf Oxen, and Goates, facies tibi boues cum hircis. In the Ghoſpell alſo, I doe (ſaith Chriſte) my Paſſouer with thee, that is, I offer vp.

Beſides al this, our Sauiour wanted not to shewe vs the matter of our Sacrifice, and $\tilde{y}$ externe things to the ſame apperteining, as the Chalice, and the Table, which had then the place, and was in ſtede of the Altar, as hereafter shall be declared by S. Paule. Of the which things may moſt plainly be gathered the definition of the Sacrifice of the Altar, that is to witte, what thing (according to his owne proper ſubſtance) is that, whiche $\tilde{y}$ Chriſtians do cal the Maſſe.

The Sacrifice therefore of

Exod. 29
Leuit. 23
Num. 15.
Iudic. 29.
13. Ezec.
43, 46.

C v　　the

In Pſ.65.
Matt.26.
Heb.vlt.
Definit-
tio miſſę
Athanaſ.
ad Antio
quęſt.34.

the Altar (which otherwiſe is
called the Maſſe) is a comme=
moration of the death and paſ=
ſion of Chriſt , by whoſe com=
maundement bread and wine
are therein conſecrate, and vn=
der the ſignes and forme of the
ſelfe ſame bread & wine , is the
very bodie and bloude of our
Sauiour Chriſte both really
preſent, and alſo offered vp vn=
to God the Father for the ſal=
uation of the world, as wel for
the glorie of God , as alſo the
ioye and comforte of the vni=
uerſal Church, and they are re=
ceaued no leſſe for the reſection
of our ſoules, then for a pledge
of the reſurrection of our bo=
dies. when I ſay, for the ſaluation of the world, I vnderſtãd
for the liue and dead: and when
I ſay, the Church, I mean not
only this Militant, but alſo the
Triumphant. For there is no
doubt, but, if it conforme it ſelf
with

with the wil of God (to whoſe honour this Sacrifice is done) it ſelf ſhal alſo feele moſt great ioye and côſolation in ſo great an offering.

The Sacrifice of the Altar is shewed by S. Paule as well by the cháge of the old Prieſthod, and by the things which are côuenient vnto a true Sacrifice, as alſo bicauſe by it is expelled Idolatrie and al falſe worshipping of God.

Cap. V.

Saint Paule writing to the Hebrewes, ſaith : Yf the full ende and conſummation was by the Prieſthoode of the Leuites (bycauſe the people receaueth the Lawe vnder it) wherefore was it neſarie, to haue an other Prieſthod, which ſhuld be called after ẙ order of Melchiſedech, not after

Heb. 7.

ter the order of Aaron? For the
Priesthod being transferred, it
was also necessarie, that $\flat$ Law
should be transferred. The re-
probation of the former Law,
was therfore vndoutedly don,
bycause it was weake and vn-
profitable : for $\flat$ Law brought
nothing to perfection. And
hervpon the blessed Apostle
S. Paule (for the better intro-
duction of a more assured and
greater hope, by the which we
may approche & draw neare to
God) sheweth in these words,
that Christ changing his Olde
Priesthod, did establish $\flat$ New
of $\flat$ new Law, which is much
perfecter then the Olde. For
Priesthod is in such sort linked
& connexed to $\flat$ Law, $\flat$ trans-
ferring the one, the other must
nedes be transferred, & establi-
shing the one, the other necessarily must wal be established.
wherof it foloweth, that the
new

new Lawe coulde not stand, if this Sacrifice wer taken from it. without this order of priesthood (saith Ignatius ye scholer of S. Iohn the Euangelist) is neither Churche elect, neither any Comunion or felowship of Saintes, neither any holie congregation. S. Paule himselfe sheweth, that the things, which doe appertaine to a true Sacrifice, are in our Table, ye is, in the Altar: as he declareth to the Hebrews.

Epist. 2. ad Tralk.

First, he exhorteth the Corinthians, to make no Sacrifice vnto the Diuels, bycause it is idolatrie, but to participate of the most blessed Sacrament of the Altar, where they may be partakers of Christ himself. As vnto wise and prudent men (saith he) I speake: be ye your selues iudges of that I saie. The Chalice of benediction, which we do blesse, is it not a

1.Cor.10.

cont-

A Treatise of the

communicating of the bloud of
Christ? The bread, which we
do breake, is it not a participa=
tion of the bodie of our Lord?

Chrysost
hom 2.
in c.5. ad
Rom.

And anon after he sheweth,
that through this our Sacri=
fice is Idolatrie auoided, and
that the Sacrifice of the beasts,
which truely (although carnal=
ly) was offered of the Iewes,
might wel admonish & warne
vs, that as they by eating of the
hostes, and offeringes of their
Altars were made partakers
of the Sacrifices therof : so we
by participating of this better
host, are made partakers & cõ=
municantes of this pure & ho=
ly Sacrifice, and therfore con=
sequently addeth: See and be=
holde Israell according to the
flesh, that is, according to the
manner of the carnall Sacrifi=
ces of that Iudaical l people.
They which do eate of the hosts,
that is, of the Sacrifices, are
they

they not partakers of ẙ Altar?
But what? Do I ſaie, ẙ that,
which is offered vp to Idols,
is any thing? Oʒ that ẙ Idol
it ſelf is any thing? Rather do
I affirme, that ẙ things which
the Gentiles do offer, are ſuch
things as they offer vnto the
Diuels, and not vnto God. I
wil not therfoʒe, that ye be the
companions of the Diuelles.
Ye can not dʒinke the Chalice
of the Loʒd, and the Chalice of
the Diuel: Ye can not be par=
takers both of the Table, that
is, the Altar of the Loʒd, & alſo
of that of the Diuelles.

   Al theſe things S. Auſtine,
and befoʒe him S. Chʒyſoſtom
do ſhew, ẙ they appertaine to
ẙ Sacrifice of the Chʒiſtiã Al=
tar, in ẙ which we haue ẙ Ob=
lation, ẙ Côſecration, ẙ Bodie
& bloud of Chʒiſt, ẙ Table, the
Chalice, the Participation, that
is, the eating: in ẙ which moſt
abſo=

Li. côtra
aduerſar.
Leg. &
Prophet.
c. 19. In. 1.
a.l Co. 10
Aug. lib.
20. côtra
Fauſt.
cap. 21.

absolute and most perfect Sacrifice we serue and adore the true God, as the Gentiles in their most wicked sacrifice did committe idolatrie, and serue the Diuell.

By the Altar, which the Apostles vsed, and after them the whole auncient Churche, is proued the Christian Sacrifice. Cap. VI.

Heb. vlt.

WE haue (saieth S. Paule) an Altar, of the which they can not eate, which doo serue the Tabernacle, that is, which do serue the sacrifices of brute beasts, & of other things in the Lawe of Moyses, the which sacrifices were all taken away by $\hat{y}$ of the Crosse, wherof this Sacrifice, of the whiche we nowe entreate, taketh his whole force and efficacie. And there

therfore he that thinketh to remaine stil (as S. Paule meaneth, in those things of y Olde
Temple) beleeueth not in the
Messias, which hath made an
ende of those shadowes, and
therefore can he not yet participate of the Christian Altar.
Our Sauiour likewise geuing
a Law of pacifying and recon-
ciling vs with our enemie, the
whiche apperteined not vnto
them of the Olde Testament,
which had his ende, but vnto
vs of the New, made mention
of the Altar, vppon the whiche
he commaunded that none such
should offer any oblatiõ, which
was at variance or contention
with his neighbour, vnlesse he
wer first recõciled vnto y same.

Primasius a Cõmenter of y
Apocalipse, writing vpon these
wordes: Measure the Temple,
and the Aultar, and them that
adore in it, interpreteth y Altar
for

Primas.
lib.2. in
Apoc.

for the Priests, and the Temple
for the faithfull, conformably
vnto that saying of S. Paule:
Ye are the Temple of God, &
ye holy Ghost dwelleth in you.
Besides this, the Altar (which
in the Greeke tongue in ye Epistle to the Hebrews is called ye
Sacrificatorie) doth expressely
signifie, that wher an Altar is,
there ought Sacrifices both to
be offred, sanctified, & also con-
serued. As touching to be offered, Germanus ye Archebishop
of Costantinople saith: The Altar is a Propitiatorie, in the
which offerings are made for
our sinnes, according to ye holy
record of Christ, who also vpo
the Altar presented him selfe in
Sacrifice vnto God his Father, by the meanes of ye Oblation of his blessed Bodie.

As concerning to be sanctified, our Lord said fitly to that
purpose: whether is greater, ye
gift, or els ye Altar, which doth

De My-
stica The
olog.

Matt. 23.

sanctifie the gifte? speaking of the oblations which ÿ Iewes made. Finally for ÿ conseruing of Sacrifices, Philo doth declare, saying: that the Altar is called a conseruatorie or a custodie of Sacrifices. Dionisius ÿ Disciple of S. Paul, Ignatius, Cyprian, Ambrosius, & S. Austine, besides many others, both of the Greeke and Latine Church, do make most manifest mentiõ of this perpetual vse of ÿ Altar, which hath ben receaued of ÿ Apostles, after ÿ institution of our Sauiour Christ.

Philo. li. 3 de vita Moysi. De Eccl. Hier. c. 3. ep. 3. ad Trall. li. 4. ep. 9 ad Florē.

Christ him self is present in the holy Sacrament of the Altar.

Cap. VII.

OVr Sauiour said with his holy woord, which shal continew for euer: *Isai. 4○.* This is my bodie, this is my bloud. And his will was, ÿ three Euãgelists should vv the very same words expresse ÿ self same

same veritie, to the ende (saith he) that as the veritie consisteth
in the mouth and testimonie of

Matt.18.

two or three , so may it also be assuredly beleued . He addeth for a fourth testimonie s. Iohn

Ioan.6.

the Euangelist, and for the fift S. Paule. and last of al for the

1.Cor.10. & 11.

sixth,the consent and vniuersal faith as well of the East and African Churche,as also of the west : that is, both the Greke Church and Latine.

Matt.26.

S. Matthew saith : whiles they were at Supper, Iesus toke bread and blessed, & brake, & gaue to his Disciples,saying Take and eate,this is my bodie. And after taking the Chalice, gaue thanks, and reached it to them, saying : Drinke ye all of this , for this is my bloude of the Newe Testamente , the which for you & for many shall be shedde for the remission of

Mar.14.

sinnes, S. Marke hath also no

lesse

leſſe then this, and that euen in
a māner, in ẙ ſelf ſame woꝛds.
S. Luke after him wꝛiteth in
this ſoꝛte : And Ieſus hauing
taken bꝛead, gaue thanks, and
bꝛake , and gaue to them, ſay=
ing : This is my Body which
is geuē foꝛ you. Do ye this foꝛ
the remembꝛance of me : and
likewiſe the Chalice, after he
had ſupt, ſaying : This is the
Chalice, the New Teſtament
in my bloude, whiche ſhall be
ſhed foꝛ you. And S. Paule,
bycauſe(ſaith he)I haue recea=
ued of our Loꝛde that , whiche
withall I ſhewed you , that is
to witte, that our Loꝛd Ieſus
in the night , wherein he was
betrayed,toke bꝛead , and ren=
dꝛing thankes, bꝛake and ſaid:
Take,⁊ eate, this is my bodie,
which ſhalbe geuen foꝛ you:do
ye this foꝛ the memoꝛie of me.
And in like manner ẙ Chalice
after he had ſupt, ſaying:This
Chalice

Luc.22.

1.Cor.11.

Chalice is the new Testament
in my bloud: Do ye this, so of=
ten as ye drinke, for the remem
brance of me.

The veritie that is gathered out
of the aforesaid Testimo-
nies. Cap. VIII.

Historia.
Prima
veritas.

First and principally, we
see, $\bar{y}$ wheresoeuer $\bar{y}$ Eua=
gelists are so curiouse and
diligent to repeate, almost
ech one $\bar{y}$ very self same words,
that there is some thing decla=
red according to $\bar{y}$ very truth
therof, and historically, not in a
similitude or in parable. For $\bar{y}$
parables which one Euange=
list reciteth, are commonly ei=
ther of the others expounded
after the true sence and signifi=
cation, vnto the whiche they
were applied, or at the least
interpreted of our Saniour
Christ himselfe.

Secunda
veritas.

Besides this we do vniuer=
sally

ſally beleue (as wee are bound
to do)that in theſe wordes is a
moſt excellent Sacramēt inſtituted. wherof we may cōclude,
ẏ thoſe viſible ſignes of bread
and wine, which are preſented Sacra-
vnto vs, are holie ſignes of mentū.
ſome thing reallie conteined
vnder them: the which thing if
we demaund the queſtion of
our Lord Ieſus Chriſt, what
thing it is, he anſwereth vs
plainely by the voice of his
Euangeliſtes, and Apoſtles:
This is my Bodie, this is my
bloud.

we ought therefore to geue
credite vnto him, who is the
veritie and truth it ſelfe, and Ioan.14.
to captiuate our witte and vnderſtanding to the obedience 2.Cor.10
and obſequie of him: knowing
that ſith our faith is by hearing Rom.10
the worde of God, if we will at
any time intermeddle or put in
eyther the ſence of touching,
O₂

or of tasting, or seing $ things
which to faith onely do apper=
taine, we shalbe alwaies fow=
ly deceiued : forasmuch as the
Diuine operations of God are
not measured wt any humaine
reason or iudgement, but with
the liuely knowledge of God,
which onely is gotten by faith,

Heb.11.

as the which is (saith S. Paul)
an argumente of thinges in=
uisible.   Moreouer whereas
this is a Sacrament of $ New
Law, it ought not to be onely
a naked and simple signe, but
to bring wt it some truth prefi=
gured before in the Old Testa=

Heb.10.
Heb.7.

ment, as wel bycause $ Law of
Moyses had only $ shadowes
of perfections to come, and it

Ioan.1.
In prœ.
exposit:
Psal.73.

selfe brought nothing to per=
fection, as also for that grace
and truth ought to be made by
our Lord and redemer. wher=
vpon S. Augustine saith, the
sacramentes of the Old Lawe
                                    did

did only promiſe ſaluation, and
ours of the newe doo geue it.
wee now therefore doo really
receaue the true meate, that is,
the very fleſh of Ieſus Chriſt,
and together therwithal, grace
and benediction of God, if we
duely prepare our ſelues worthily to comunicate of ý ſame:
whereas in the Old Law, the
Iewes receaued the ſelfe ſame
meate onely ſpiritually, as S.
Paule declareth. And albeit
they were fedde with Manna,
yet they receaued no more but
Chriſte in a figure. For ſo did
Melchiſedech (of whome wee
ſpake before) vſe bread & wine,
in a figure only: but our Lord,
and we (through his infinite
goodneſſe) do vſe it in the veritie. The Iewes were baptiſed in a clowd, and in the ſea:
but we truly are baptiſed with
water, & with the holy Ghoſt.
The Iewes offered Oxen and

Ioan.6.

Ioã.6.&
1.Cor.10.

1.Cor.10

Ioan.6.

Gen.14.

1.Cor.10.

Ioan.3.

D　　Lambes:

Calues: but wee doe offer the bodie and bloud of our Lorde. The Moisaical Priests did respect the leaprie of the flesh, & did procure to purge the same with Olde Sacrifices, & other ceremonies: but the Christian Priestes do looke to the sinnes of the soule, and in the vertue of the holie Ghost doo remitte them.

Moyses saw ẙ burning flame, whiche did not consume: the Blessed Virgin Marie came, & conceaued, & brought forth the true light & splendour of ẙ Father, and yet remained neuerthelesse a most pure & immaculate Virgin. water issued forth of ẙ rocke in wildernesse: both water and bloud issued out of the side of our Sauiour Iesus Christ. Those Hebrews drank the liquor of the rocke, which vnto them signified Christe: but we doo drinke the true liquor

Margin notes:

Ambros. li.1.off.
Leuit.13. & 14.

Ioan,20. & Matt. 16.18.
Exod.3.

Ioan.1.

Heb 1.

Num.20

quoꝛ of the true Jesus Chꝛiste, Ioan.16.
the whiche commeth not after 1.Cor.10.
vs (as one that shoulde come
to geue vs the truth, as the
Jewes looked foꝛ) but is really pꝛesent with vs.

The thirde veritie which is Tertia
gathered of these Euangelists, veritas.
is, that whereas the thing it
selfe is geuen to vs, whereby
the Testamente is confirmed :
it muste by all reason needes
bee, that the Testatoꝛ wante
not to expounde plainely his
will and pleasure of the same. Testa-
Foꝛ as muche as therefoꝛe our mentū.
Sauiour leafte vs a moste effectuall meanes to remayne
liuely vnited with him, and a
moste liuelie memoꝛie of the
death which he suffered foꝛ vs,
the which of our boūden dutie
we ought continually to haue
befoꝛe our eyes : it can not be,
but that without all doubte he
leaft vs also the things moste 1.Cor.10.
　　　　　　D ij　　　plaine

plaine and manifest of that his
said wil and Testament: especially sith the same was endi-
ted and written by most authen
tique and faithfull Notaries,
which wanted not to all faith-
fulnesse, diligence, and solem-
nitie, to take in writing that,
which was committed to them,
without altering one iote of
the true sence and meaning of
the same.

Præceptū

This being done, our Lord
gaue vs after in commaunde-
ment, what he would haue vs
to doe with that his most blessed and pretiouse Bodie, which
is, to vse it for a memorie of the
death of him, by offering it vp
vnto the eternall Father, not
only for a thanks geuing, neither yet for an onely remembrance, but also for our saluation, which is the frute of this
remembrance. Now this com-
maundemente and precept of
our

1. Cor. 11.

our Sauiour geuen to vs concurring with the inſtitution & other things, wherof we ſpake before, we may therof be wel aſſured, ẙ they can doo no leſſe, but declare vnto vs a ſimple & plaine veritie, which may illuminate our hartes to geue credite therein to the true & only begotten Sonne of God. The precept (ſaith Dauid) of our Lord is bright and lightſome, and doth illuminate our eyes.

Pſal. 18.

Our Lord ſaith: Do ye this: what (I pray you) is it, that they muſt doo? It is not, to make ẙ bread, for it was made before: neither the wine, which was then in his perfect ſtate & being: neither was it only to do the effect of eating & drinking, for they had done that in the Paſchal Lambe. what then was it that our Sauiour bade them to doe? Truely the ſelfe ſame thing that he did, who by

D iij   his

his blessing chãged and trans=
muted this material bread into
his prettiouse bodie.

Quarta
veritas.
Besides this, wheras Christ
spake so sincerely and plainly,
that he gaue vs that bodie and
that bloud, which on the tree
of the Crosse shoulde purchace
vnto vs the remission of our
sinnes: it is without al doubt,
that he gaue vs not bread, but
his owne very Bodie. For
otherwise should we saie, that
not he, but the bread was cru=
cified for vs: which is a most
impiouse and a blasphemouse
thing, not onely to be saied,
but also to be imagined of any
Christian man.

The Testimonie of S. Iohn
the Euangelist.

Cap. IX

Ioan. 6.
THe holic Ghoste did also
vse a maruelous way and
meanes in causing s. Iohn
the Euangelist to write of this
veritie.

veritie. Foʒ he pʒoueth it with
two miracles, and with one fi=
gure, and alſo with a leſſon oʒ
ſermõ of our Sauiour Chʒiſt.

The firſt miracle was, that
with fiue barley loaues & two
fiſſhes he fedde fiue thouſand
perſons. Foʒ after he had ge=
uen thankes (ſaith the Euan=
geliſt) he cauſed the ſaid meate
& bʒead to be diſtributed emõg
geſt them : who being all ſatiſ=
ſied therof, ẏ Apoſtles gathered
vp twelue baſkets oʒ coffines
ful of the leauings & fragmẽts
of the ſame. Hereof we haue to
vnderſtand, ẏ as he fed ſo great
a multitude with ſo litle meate
& ſuſtenance, and yet ſo muche
therof remained in fragments:
euen ſo (foʒ as muche as the
bʒead was in the hands of him
that did diſtribute it, & yet the
multitude was really fed of ẏ
ſame) the Apoſtles (being ad=
uertiſed of ſo great a myſterie)
　　　　D iiij　　　ought

ought not afterwardes doubt,
but that our Lord himself gaue
them his true and reall Bodie,
although they sawe it presente
before them, & heard him saying : Take, this is my Bodie:

In Pf. 33. ý which (saith S.Austine) was
then caried of our Lord in his
owne handes, when he did distribute it vnto his Disciples.

The seconde miracle was,
that he walked vppon the sea,
and made the shippe sodainely
arriue to the sea banke . The
which things did serue well to
instruct his Disciples , and the
selfe same multitude of people
which folowed him, to beleeue
that he was not onely a man,
but God also , and therefore
could be where it pleased him,
without the lette or hindrance
of any corporal thing . Al this
did also very wel make for the
declaration of that whiche the
Capharnaites after (through
their

their infidelitie) vnderſtoode
not, in that thei thought to eate
(as S. Auſtine ſaith) only the In Ioã.6.
fleſh of a bare man, like that of
the boutchers ſhambles : no=
thing at al conſidering y̑ ſpirit
of his Diuinitie, by the vertue
wherecof, the Bodie of Chriſte
himſelfe ought to be taken re=
ally of vs, to quicken and re=
niue vs by the ſame.

After theſe two miracles, the
Euangeliſt maketh mentiõ of
the figure, which our Sauiour
declared befoꝛe he pꝛeached of y̑
verity of his body, which ſhuld
be our meate. That figure was
Mãna, which deſcẽded frõ hea=
uen : that Mãna, ſaith he, gaue
not true life, but the bꝛead that
deſcended from heauẽ gaue it,
which was the Godhead itſelf,
and ſpirit of God. Now after
our Loꝛd had thus declared his
Godhead, he afterward ſhew=
eth, that not onely he woulde
            D v   geue

geue vs his spirite to bee our
meate and sustenance, but that
withal we shuld also haue his
verie bodie and bloud to eate:
and therefore after he had said:
I am the breade of lyfe whiche
descended from heauen : hee
addeth : and the breade whiche
I shall geue, is my flesh for the
life of the worlde : Uerely, ve=
rely I saie vnto you, if ye eate
not the flesh of the Sonne of
manne, and drinke his bloud,
ye shall not haue lyfe in you.
Hee that eateth my flesh, and
drinketh my bloude hath lyfe
euerlastinge. My fleshe is
truely meate, and my bloude
is truely drinke. Hee that
eateth my flesh, and drinketh
my bloude, remaineth in me,
and I in him. As my liuing
Father sente mee, and I liue
for my Father: so he that ea=
teth me, shall liue for me.

Of

Of these woordes of our Sauiour didde the vnfaithfull moze hardenne their heartes, then befoze they were: and therefoze oure Lozde addeth moreouer: Doth this offend you? what then if yee shall see the Sonne of manne ascende vppe, where he was befoze? That is to saie, if yee dooe not nowe beleeue, that ye may here in the earth feede your selues wyth my fleshe: howe will yee beleeue it heereafter, at that tyme when yee shal see, that I haue visibly taken my selfe out of your presence, and shall from heauen (as Saint Athanasius saieth) geaue vnto the worlde this selfe same flesh of myne, being then made spirituall and Celestial? (that is to saie, glozified) And foz this cause it foloweth:

Athanas.
de verbis
Euang.
Quicunque dix-
erit ver-
bum in
Spirit. S.

The

The spirite and the Diuinitie (which you beleue not to be in me) is that whiche geueth life: the flesh helpeth not a whitte. Which is as muche to say, as this: Although the flesh it self be really receaued, yet vnlesse wee beleeue in the Godheade which is in the same, & whence lyfe principallye redoundeth vnto vs, it auayleth vs nothing at all. For euen many euil and wicked men (saith S. Augustine) do receaue the flesh and bloud of Christ in the Sacramēt: but this is not enough. For bysides this, it behooueth vs also, to ioyne and vnite our spirit with the spirit of God, & to remaine firme and stedfast in him, and in his holie faith, and in all good woorkes, like members in one bodie, if wee wil with due frute and vtilitie, receaue so pretiouse a meate.

These were ÿ woordes which Christ

Tract. 27 in Ioan.

Christ spake, & they were true=
ly spirit and life. wherefore the
Capharnaites oughte not to
haue fixed their thoughtes and
cogitations onely in the flesh,
but to haue penetrated into p
Godhead : p which if they had
beleeued, they had not concea=
ued a wrong and sinister mea=
ning of his wordes, to whome
nothing is impossible. It be=
houeth vs therfore, to beleue &
gene credite to Iesus Christe.
For who so euer denyeth, that
he geueth vs his flesh, denyeth
God himselfe, which dwelling
& inhabiting in him woorketh
this miraculouse and wonder=
ful operation.

The Testimonie of S. Paule.

Cap. X.

THe Chalice (saieth S. ¹·Cor.¹⁰
Paule) which we blesse,
is it not a communica=
ting of p blud of Christ ?
And

Ioan.6.

and the bread which we break, is it not a participation of the bodie of Chzifte? And in the next Chapter folowing, he addeth: He that shall eate this Breade (vnderstandinge for Bread that, which he declared to be his flesh) and shal dzinke this Cuppe of the Lozde vnwozthily, shall be gyltie of the bodie and bloud of our Lozde. And he addeth the cause why he shall becomme giltie thereof: whiche is, bycause he doth not discerne the Bodie of our Lozde. As though he had said, bycause he will iudge that to be bread, which after the Consecration is made the very bodie of Chzift.

He sheweth after, howe God dothe punnish and chasten them, which without pzouinge them selues, that is, without good examination of their faith and conscience, goe to re=

to receaue this blessed meate.
whereuppon he saith : Many
of you are founde to bee in=
firme and weake : that is, ma=
ny of you (through so wic=
ked and enormiouse sinne) are
lame and maymed : and many
do sleepe, which is to saie, die.

He that therefore will dili=
gently obserue, howe greate a
punnishmente this is, whiche
here our Lord threateneth, and
withal wil consider, that proper=
ly a man is to be said debtour,
and giltie of that, which really
he hath receaued : shall plaine=
ly see, how plaine and expresse
a testimonie of the truth this
is, whiche that moste blessed
Vessell of Christe S. Paule
dooth heere alleage : who fur=
ther, speaking of the participa=
tion of the Body and bloud of
Christe, and not onely of the
spirite of God (the whiche is
well knowen neuer to departe
                         from

Ignat.in
epistola
adSmyr-
nen.citã-
te Theo-
dorito.
Dialog.3
In vita
Moseos.
Contra
Nestoriũ
Chryf. in
Psal.50.
Idem. in
1.Cor.10.
Origen.
in Num.
hom.7.
Apolo.2.
Theoph.
in 26.c.
Matth.
Athanaf.
de verbis
Euang.
Quicun-
que dix-
erit ver-
bum in
Spirit. S.

from thofe moft glozious mem
bers (& bleffed Boðie of Chzift)
doth thereby conclude, that the
pure wozde of God, ought not
herein to be in any cafe other=
wife vnderftood.

The Teftimonies of certayne
principall auncient Fathers
of the Eaft Church.

Cap. XI.

IGnatius wziting of thys
moft holy Sacrament, faith:
that it is þ flefh of our Bleffed Sauiour, which fuffered
foz our finnes, whom þ celeftial
Father (of his benignitie) rei=
fed frõ death to life. S. Gzego-
rie Nyffene calleth it a wozke,
which neither ploughing, nei=
ther fowing, but þ only Sonne
of God, hath pzepared foz vs.
A bzead, in the which (wziteth
Cyzill) God hath infufed the
power of life, which is the true
and bleffed flefhe of the liuely
wozðs

worde it ſelfe : Ful of life, ſaith Chryſoſtome, & with him Origen : The fleſh of the Incarnate, ſaith Iuſtine, the whiche albeit it ſeemeth bread, yet is it the bodie of Chriſt : & the fleſh of ẙ ſame (as witneſſeth Theophilacte) the which is the preſeruation and conſeruatorie of life , to riſe to lyfe euerlaſting (ſaith Athanaſius) and finally it is a Bodie endewed with Godhead, as Damaſcene concludeth.

The Chalice of the Euchariſt or Sacrifice of ẙ Altar (ſaith Dionyſius) is a ſingular Chalice, dreadfull and terrible, the whiche excelleth the Diuine, & Angelical nature, and ẙ which is adorned with al vertue (ſaith S. Chryſoſtome) where is the bloud of the New Teſtament, not of the Olde, ſaieth Euthymius.

Damaſ.
li. 4 c 14.
in Eccleſ.
Hierar.
Hom. 84
in Io. &
Hom. ad
baptizá-
dos &
hom. 24.
1. Cor. 10.
Euthy 26
cap Mat.
Contra
Ioui li. 1.
Hilar. in
Pſal. 127.
Bernard.
Ser 1. in
vig. Nat.
Dom.
De ijs q
myſterijs
initiátur.
cap. 9.
Hilar. in
Pſal. 64.
Bed. hiſt .
li. 1. c. 27.

The

A Treatise of the

The Testimonies of certaine principall Writers of the West Church.

Cap. XII.

Hieron.
contra
Ioui.li.2.
Ambrof.
cap.1.ad
Cor. 11..
ad id
mortem
Dom.an
nuntiam
Pfal.80.
De facra
li.4.c.9.

Saint Ierome, & S. Hilarie do cal this blessed Sacramente, that selfe same Bread, whiche descended from heauen: and the whiche (after the consecration and sanctification thereof) is now no more a figure of ye Body of our Lord, but ye very blessed Bodie it self of Christ: neither is it a figure of the flesh of our Sauiour, but his owne proper & true flesh. For it is that (saith S. Ambrose) which the benediction hath consecrated, with the which benediction euen nature it selfe is also changed. It is the meate, by the which wee are saued, and in the which the word is made flesh. Finally it is the Diuine flesh, & pretiouse
Bodie

Bodie of our Loꝛde Omnipo=
tent. It is that (ſaith S. Je=
rome) which both the good &
the euill doe a like receaue , al=
though with farre vnlike frute
and pꝛofitte.

In like ſoꝛte S. Ambꝛoſe
ſpeaking of the cuppe oꝛ Cha=
lice, calieth it ẏ ſelf ſame bloud,
which was offered vp foꝛ vs :
ẏ ſame (ſaith Arnobius) which
ẏ cruel Jewes dꝛew of Chꝛiſt,
and which hath redeemed the
people, and was ſhed (wꝛiteth
S. Jerome) foꝛ the remiſſion of
our ſinnes.

The Teſtimonies of certayne
    principal Fathers of the
        African Church.

Cap. XIII

WE eate (ſaieth Ter=
tullian) the fleſhe,
and wee dꝛinke the
bloud of Chꝛiſte, to
the entente our ſowle may be
                    made

Tertull.
de reſur.
corp.
Cypr de
cœn. D.
ibidem.
Ad Ian.
epiſt. 118.
& Ter-
tull. ad
vxor.
Contra
Palm. l. 6
Aug ad
Caſul.
epiſt. 96.

made fatte with God. And this
is that bread and wine, whiche
can not bee consumed of any
multitude. It is this (saieth
Cyprian) into whiche the Di=
uine essence is infused. To this
bodie (saith S. Augustine) hath
this honour and reuerence ben
geuen of the vniuersal Church
by the instruction of the holie
Ghost, that it should first enter
into a Christian mans mouth,
before any other external mea=
tes doo enter into him. With
whiche meate is the Chalice,
which our Lord left vs, wher=
in is carried (saith Optatus)
the bloud of Christe. This is
the Chalice, in the which is the
bloud, wherwith we haue ben
redeemed and made the liuely
members of God: the bloud,
I saie, that is the moste blessed
and pretiouse drinke that is,
whiche beeing receaued of the
heart and mouth of the good
and

Cyp.ep 3
lib.3.
Aug.cõt.
Cret.li.4
cap.19.
Contra
aduersar.
Leg. &
Prophet.
l.2 c.9.
& ad Ian.
epist.118.

and faithfull, is for their salua=
tiõ, and washing away of their
sinnes: but being receaued of
the vnworthy mouth of ẙ vn=
faithfull and wicked, it is (as
witnesseth S. Augustine) to
them for their iudgemẽt, death
and condemnation. The Be= Nicen.
neral Councell of Nice, with Concil.
such others, do call it the meate Ephef.
not of sacietie, but of sanctimo= Symbol.
nie, which is the proper fleshe Ephe.
of ẙ very worde, the flesh that Nicen.1.
geueth life, the necessary way= can.12.
faring meate, & the blessed Bo= Concil.
die of our Redemer.   Ephef

Certaine aduertisementes concerning the trueth of the
blessed Sacrament.

Cap. XIIII.

Bycause in the Sacramẽts
is both the signe, and also
the thing it selfe that is si=
gnified by ẙ signe: thereof
it com=

it commeth, ꝩ sometimes this
blessed Sacramēt is called by ꝩ
name of a signe and figure : as
in speaking of the outwarde
shape and externe forme which
we see with our corporal eyes.
Neuerthelesse we may not inferre thereof, but that the holie Doctours doo alwaies vnderstande, vnder that figure
and signe to be conteined that,
whiche the mouth of our Sauiour pronounced to be there
presente : that is to saie, hys
owne venerable and glorious
Bodie : which also in the Gospell was of olde Symeon called a signe, against which, con-
tradiction shoulde be made.

Againe, bycause the true
Bodie of our Lorde is a Figure and a Signe of the vnitie of Christes Churche, for
this cause also dothe S. Augustine, and others of the Doctours, oftentimes thus call
it:

it : to shewe thereby the diui=
sion of the Donatistes and o=
ther Heretiques, whiche haue
not the vnitie that is signified
by this Bodie of Christe, by=
cause they are diuided and se=
parate from the Church.

Nowe when S. Augustine
also saith, that it is an impiouse
thing, to imagine to eate the
flesh of Christe fleshly and car=
nally : he is there to be vnder=
stood, to speake onely of them,
which (after the manner of the
Capharnaites) beleeued to
teare (saith S. Augustine) the
blessed fleshe of Christe with
their teeth, one member from
an other, none otherwise then
they doo with the flesh of the
shambles.

So likewise is this Blessed
Sacramēt called bread, bicause
bothe the Hebrewes, and also
holie Scriptures do vnderstād
by the name of bread, not only
the

the bread ꝑ is made of wheate,
but also flesh, and generally al
kindes of meate and substance.
& yet is it neuer declared, what
thing this bread is after Con=
secration, but that it is expresly
called the very flesh and Bodie
of Chrift.

As touching the Article of
the Creede, whiche hath, that
our Lorde afcended vnto the
right hand of the Father, and
from thêce shal come to iudge
the quicke and the dead, which
Article, bycaufe it feemeth to
fome mê to make fome fcruple
and difficultie : ye shal vnder=
ftande, that it maketh nothing
at all againft the veritie of the
prefence of Chrifte in the Sa=
crament of the Altar. For the
Angelles them felues haue de=
clared, in what forte the lafte
cõming of our Sauiour Chrift
shall bee vnto the vniuerfall
Iudgement : which is, that he
shal

ſhal come viſibly , & in the ſelfe
ſame forme and manner as he
aſcended vppe vnto the trium=
phant heauen, his Apoſtles be=
holding and waiting on him.
This his laſt cōming doth no=
thing at all derogate from his
ſecrete and hidden preſence vn=
der the holie ſignes of bread &
wine in the Sacrament: ſith
the manner of appearance is
diuerſe , as alſo it was, when
our Lord (notwithſtanding he
was aſcended into heauen) yet
ſhewed himſelfe to S. Paule,
recalling him frō his Iudaiſme

In like manner the ſitting
of Chriſt at the right hande of
the Father , doth neither more
nor leſſe lette or hinder his pre=
ſence in the bleſſed Sacramēt:
bycauſe in this his bleſſed pre=
ſence, the body of Chriſt (which
alwayes is vnited to his Di=
uinitie) hath the propertie of a
Diuine being : which is, to be
　　　　　E　　　　wholy

wholy in heauen, and wholy in euery cōsecrated hoste, without either moouing oʒ changing it selfe in any point.

The Bodie then of Chʒiste (whiles it sitteth on the right hande of his Father, that is, in the Maiestie and gloʒie of God) is not in such oʒder and natural foʒme in the holie Sacrament, as by common course of nature elsewhere other bodies are : but it is there pʒesent by his Diuine propʒietie, after a way and meanes that to man is incompʒehensible. Foʒasmuch as it is not possible ne lawfull foʒ vs to reache by natural argumentes, vnto the knowledge of the moste high and supernaturall secretes of God: as also we cannot by any sense oʒ iudgement of ours vnderstand, how Chʒist did penetrate the walles to come in, the dooʒes being shut, nother how

he-

he walked on the sea, nor how
hee was nowe in Ierusalem,
now in Emaus, nor how hee
transfigured himself before his
Disciples, nor finally how he
ascended by his owne proper
vertue and force vnto heauen,
notwithstanding the naturall
weight and ponderositie of bo=
dies, and thickenesse of walles,
being a thing most vnpossible
by nature, y̌ two bodies should
at one time, be found both pre=
sent in one place.

But al this did our Sauiour
through the meanes of his Di=
uinitie, whiche incomparably
passeth the force and power of
nature: and therfore he is said
to haue a bodie which is spiri=
tual, as we also shal haue (saith
S. Paule) after our resurectiō. **1.Cor.15.**
For although we shal then re=
sume & take againe y̌ selfe same
bodie, which wee haue at this
present: yet then shal the spirit
                E ij   pre=

preuaile aboue the flesh, and by
the gift of glorificatiõ this our
bodie shall no more haue that
qualitie of corruption, neither
of heauines, whiche nowe it
hath, neither shall any suche
thing let or hinder it, but that
it may freely obey and followe
the minde, which is illustrate
and lightened with the diuine
beames of God.

Now as concerning that al=
so, ỹ which our Sauiour said:
Do ye this for the remẽbrance
of me, wherof it may perhaps
seeme, that this memorie doth
exclude the presence of the Bo=
die of Christ: we must vnder=
stand, that this memory which
we make, is not of the Bodie
of Christe whiche is there pre=
sent, but of the death which be=
fore had ben in the same Body.
And therefore our Lorde saied
not, Do ye this in remẽbrance
of this my Bodie: but Do ye
this,

this , that is to witte, Conse=
crate this Body in remembrance
of my death, to the end that we
hauing it before our eyes, may
with more feruent affection of=
fer vp in Sacrifice to the Ce=
lestial Father that body which
suffered for to redeeme vs, and
by communicating of the same,
may receaue that lyfe , whiche
common breade can not geue
vs, but that flesh of Christ doth
geue it vs, whiche (as Cyrill
saith) not onely through loue
and affection, but naturally al=
so is vnited to vs. And what
thing (saith S. Augustine) can
be so gratefully offered , or re=
ceaued, as the flesh of our Sa=
crifice being made the Bodie
of our Priest ? And againe, we
(saieth hee) with our faithfull
harte, and with our mouth doe
receue our Lord Jesus Christ,
the Mediatour of God & man,
whiche geueth vs his flesh to
E iij   cate,

Cyril.
Alex.l.10
in Ioã.13
& li.3.in
Io.c.38.
Tom.5.
lib.4.de
Trinit.
cap.4.
Tom.6
contra
Aduersar
legis &
Prophet.
li.2.c.9.
Tom.9.
Tract 84
in Ioan.

Tom.6.
contra
Fauſt.
Manich.
li.12.c.20
cate, and his bloud to dzinke.
And in an other place (saith he)
what is ẏ Table of the mighty
but that, from whence is recca=
ued the body and bloud of him,
whiche hath beſtowed his lyfe
foz vs? And againe: with the
whiche Sacrifice the Churche
(saith he) is in this time accom
panied, whiles it dzinketh that,
which iſſued out of the bleſſed
ſide of Chziſt. He (that is, our

Ciril.lib.
12.c.58.
Lozde, saith Cyzil) geueth vs
his fleſh to touche, to the ende
that we may aſſuredly beleeue,
that he hath truely reſuſcitated
his Bodie from death to life.

InLiturg
& lib.3.
De Sacer
O miracle (saith Chzysoſtome
with Baſill) O benignitie of
God: he that ſitteth in heauen
with the Father, is handled at
the selfe same time, with the
handes of al men.

Chriſte ought to be adored in
the bleſſed Sacrament.

Foz

Cap. XV.

Orasmuch as our Lord is
both God & man, wee are
without all doubt bound,
to reuerence & adoze him,
wheresoeuer it pleaseth his Di=
uine goodnesse & omnipotêcie
to be. This bodie (saith Chry= Hom.14
sostom) the Magi did adoze, and in.1.ad
reuerence in the Manger. Yf Corinth.
then the barbarouse men did v
so great a feare, after so long &
tedious a iourney adoze it: Let
vs which bee Citizens of hea=
uen, at the leastwise solow and
imitate herein this example of
y̆ Barbarous. Thou seest it not
in the Manger, but on y̆ Altar:
noz holden in the armes of a Hom.6t.
woman, but in the handes of y̆ ad pop. 1
Priest which is present. And in Antioch
an other place: If thy garmêts lib.3. de
(saieth he) be pure and cleane, Spiritu
adoze it, and communicate. Sancto.
　To this purpose S. Ambzose cap.12.
also saith: wee adoze the flesh
　　　E iij　　of

of Chriſte in the Myſteries.
And in an other place he addeth : with how great contri-
tion of hart, with what abun-
dant fountaine of teares, with
what reuerence and feare, with
how much chaſtitie of bodie &
puritie of minde , oughte this
Myſtery to be celebrated, wher
thy fleſh is truly receaued, and
thy bloude is truely drunke,
where with ſupreme thinges
are ioyned thinges ẏ are baſe,
and humaine things with Diuine : Finally where ẏ Saints
and Angelles are preſent, and
where alſo thou thy ſelfe arte,
which arte both the Prieſt and
the Sacrifice after a manner
moſt miraculouſe & vnſpeake-
able ? who can worthily celebrate this Myſterie , if thou
God Omnipotent makeſt not
him worthy to offer it ?

S. Auguſtine ſpeaking of
the ſame matter, ſaith likewiſe:
And

De Miſſa
Pſal. 98.

And bicause he gaue vs for our saluation, his owne fleshe to eate, let no mã eat of that flesh, vnlesse he first adore it. For we do not onely not sinne by ado=ring it, but we sinne, if we ad=ore it not. And elsewhere hee sheweth, that this Sacrifice ap perteineth to that worshipping & true adoratiõ which is called Latria, & therefore he that doth not adore ẙ flesh of Christ, as he gainsaith against the worde of God, which expresly cõmaun=deth vs to adore ẙ footstoole of the feete of his Maiestie, which is the earth, that is to saie, the humanitie of Christe: so doth he committe the iniquitie and offence of that faulte (as Isi=chius writeth) which properly is against God.

Lib. 20. cap. 21. contra Faust.

Epi. 120. cap. 17. & Emissen. in 4. ho. in Pasch. psal. 98.

August. psal. 98.

li. 6. c. 22 in Leuit.

The necessitie and vtilitie of the Sacrifice of the Altar.

E v   The

Cap. XVI.

THe order whiche God
our Sauiour & Lord ke=
peth in natural & visible
thinges , is muche more
perfectly kept in things which
are spiritual & inuisible , as in
suche which are of them selues
more excellent, & by nature are
more high and single. And this
not only taketh not away any
honour from his Diuine Ma=
iestie, in that it thus woorketh
by due and conuenient meanes
most orderly, but also is an oc=
casió of his greater glorie, whi=
les he doth in this wise mani=
fest his infinit wisedom: wher=
by man (lifting vp himselfe to
the knowledge of his exceding
goodnesse) may choose and e=
lect to vse those meanes, which
haue ben of our Lord himselfe
instituted to vnite and ioyne
vs with him.

wherefore as God (although
he be

he be able, to make al y̌ things
we see, with euery litle becke
oꝛ twinckling of an eye) yet
woulde hee, that firſte the ſu=
pꝛeame element ſhoulde moue
in his courſe and circle apoin=
ted, and by the meanes and
courſe of it, ſhoulde the inflꝰ
ence of motion deſcende to
the other elementes that are
inferiour, vſinge therein the
ſelfe ſame elementes the one
as an inſtrumente vnto the o=
ther: ſo hath it pleaſed muche
moꝛe hys Diuine Maieſtie, by
meanes of our Loꝛde Ieſus
Chꝛiſte (whiche is the trueſt
firmamente, and element moſt **Heb.i.**
aboundantly full of all bꝛight=
neſſe of the heauenly Father)
to geue influence of his grace
and benediction vppon hys
bleſſed Oꝛders of Angelles,
& by them conſequently to de=
ſcend with his mercy, vertue,
& iuſtice vpon our ſpirites, not
                    diſ=

disdaining therin to vse vs also as instrumentes the one to the other: to the end that finally his desired frute of saluation may spring vp in our hartes, **1.Cor.3.** which (as S. Paule saith) are ÿ tillage, edification, & plough-ground of God.

To this our foundation let vs adde, that the Crosse, whervppon our Lord Jesus Christ suffered his bitter Passion, is the true tree of life, not that whiche was once planted in ÿ terrestriall Paradise, but that which is sette in the middest of Christes Churche: that as by eating of the tree of Paradise, was by and by geuen the vniuersal sentēce of death, so who so euer plucketh and eateth of the frute of this tree, may not die, but haue life euerlasting. Now as a tree is not therefore lesse perfecte, bycause no man eateth of the frute thereof, neither

ther a fountaine is therefore
leſſe to be accompted a foun=
taine, bycauſe no man reſortes
to drinke of it: ſo our Lorde
and Sauiour leeſeth no one
point of his greatneſſe, nother
of his merites whiche he gate
on the Croſſe, although we
nothing at all enioy the bene=
fite of the ſame. Only it is our
loſſe and dammage ſo to doo:
foraſmuch as he hath not wan=
ted alſo to inſtitute moſt ſuffi=
cient meanes, wherby we may
deriue vnto vs ý grace of that
his bleſſed Sacrifice, which he
ſuffred on the Croſſe.

The neceſſitie therfore of the
Sacrifice of the Altar, is here=
of gathered, bycauſe God doth
worke moſt ordinately, & doth
diſpoſe and geue the frutes of
his Croſſe, in ſundry & diuerſe
manners proportionally, as
we (through grace) doo either
more or leſſe approche neare to

receaue

receaue them. For as (not-
withstãding our Lord hath, as
cõcerning his part, by al right,
deserued, through ꝑ his death,
the redemptiõ not only of one
worlde, but of infinite worldes)
yet wil he not, that ꝑ shedding
of his bloud vppon the Crosse
shoulde profitte the Turkes
or other Infidelles, sith they
(through their owne defaulte)
wil not apply it to themselues
by the meanes of the Sacramente of Baptisme. And as
vnto them which of meere malice do sinne, and also willingly doo remaine in sinne, there
is (saith S. Paul) neither Host,
neither Sacrifice that can auail
them : so also vnto them, that
are now baptised, ꝑ same Passion of our Lorde auaileth nothing for the remission of their
sinnes, vnlesse it be applyed &
ministred to them by ꝑ meanes
of other Sacramentes, & especially

Heb.11.

cially by the moste blessed Sacrament of the Altar.

For whereas this Sacrifice
of the Crosse was offered vp,
not for one particular state or
Countrie, but for the whole
worlde, & besides for the soules
of them that were in Limbo Pa
trum: reason woulde, that the
frute of this vniuersal offering
should be also applyed by such
a meane, whiche were it selfe
likewise correspondente and
proportionate to the same, that
as well the whole worlde, as
also the sowles of them, which
doo satisfaction vnto the iustice of God in Purgatorie,
shoulde bee partakers of the
frute thereof. And for this
cause did the infinite wisdome
of God institute this Blessed
Sacrifice of the Aultar, the
which in that it is a Sacrifice
and an offering, generally it
helpeth all men in the vertue
of

of that bloudy Sacrifice, which was made on the Crosse: but in that it is a Sacrament, particularly, it helpeth only them, which worthily do receaue it.

For if in the Law of Moyses were Sacrifices offred vp, not onely to geue thankes in memorie of the benefites receaued, but also to pacifie y wrath of our Lord, and to make him merciful to our sinnes, and yet the same beeing offered in the faith of the Messias to come, did much helpe & auaile: how much more profitable & auailable shall this Sacramente of the Gospel be vnto vs, which euery hower do cōmitte sinne, and haue so muche neede daily to applie vnto our selues the frute of the Crosse of Christe? especially syth the Sacrifice, whiche we nowe make for the memorie of our deliuerāce out of the handes of the Diuell, is
farre

farre better & more excellent,
then that which the Hebrewes
did offer with their Paschall
Lambe, for a memorie of their
deliuerance out of the handes
of Pharao.

And therefore this offering
doth also more helpe vs, then
those Sacrifices didde helpe
them: forasmuch as we doo it
not by the commaudement of
Moyses, but by the precept of
Christ: neyther in the faith of
the Messias to come, but of our
Lorde nowe presente: neither
with the flesh of beastes, but
with the flesh of the Sonne of
God do we make this miraculouse offering and Diuine Sacrifice to the eternal Father of
Heauen in a moste sweete sa-
uour, to the end that he calling
to minde the pretiouse Death
of his onely and deere beloued
Sonne, may vouchesafe to
graunt vs the influence of the
riches

riches of his grace. Bysides
this, if Moyses, Phinees, & the
Niniuites, did pacifie God w̄
their praier, if also good works
done in a liuely faith, and with
almesdedes, do deserue (as S.
Paul witnesseth) ȳ loue & grace
of God: how can it be said, but
ȳ with the offering of ȳ death of
our Sauiour, where he is him
selfe present, & where (not for a
memorie of a promise or coue=
nant made with Abraham, but
for a remembrance of a liuely
couenāt made with Christ) our
Lorde is much more pacified, &
made merciful? Seing that by=
sides this visible Sacrifice, we
also therwith offer vp inward=
ly the sacrifice of our hartes (as
S. Austine saith) whiles we a=
gnise ourselues to be sinners, &
shew in whō we put our trust
& confidence, & from whom we
loke for ȳ merite of premissiō of
our sinnes: which is of ȳ death
of

Heb. vlt.

of Chriſt.　Heerevnto finally
may wee adde ẏ neceſſitie alſo,
which is takē of ẏ OldLaw, in
ẏ which Prieſthood was neuer
ſeparate frō ẏ doing of the com
maūᵈemēts of God: yea rather
ẏ one was alwaies imperfecte
ẃout the other. whervpō it fo=
loweth, ẏ where ẏ Law is bet=
ter (as owrs is) ther alſo muſt
cōſequently be ẏ better Sacri=
fice, ⱖ the better worſhipping
of God. And therfore (ſaith S.
Jerom) That which is wꝛiten
of ẏ people of Iſrael, that they
went foꝛth in ẏ hand of Moſes
ⱖ Aaron : vnderſtand ye it of ẏ
Law ⱖ Prieſthod of ẏ woꝛkes
ⱖ woꝛſhipping of God, the one
wherof hath nede of the other.
And after he addeth: with theſe
two hāds (as iᵗ were with two
Seraphins) we go out to con=
feſſe the holie Trinitie, ſaying :
Holie, Holie, Holie, Loꝛd God
of Sabaoth.

The

Ad Fabi-
ol. de 42
mansio-
nibus.

The Sacrifice of the Altar, in
what thing it agreeth with the
Sacrifice of the Crosse : and
how they doe muche derogate
from the honour of Christe,
which do cal it simply the Supper or meate of our Lord, without attributing vnto it the
name of an Oblation
or Sacrifice.

Cap. XVII.

THe difference that is betwene the Sacrifice of ỹ
Crosse, & the Sacrifice of
the Altar, consisteth in
two things.

Differen-
tia prima
The first is, that on ỹ Crosse
our Sauiour offered vp himselfe, to the end he might thereby purchase and get vs grace,
righteousnesse , sanctitie , and
eternal saluation, by ỹ meanes
of his death and Passion, with
the which he ouercame the Diuell and killed Death : But
in

in his laste Supper hee didde
not institute the Sacrifice or
the Oblation of the Altar, by=
cause there shoulde be a newe
Sanctification or Redemption
gotten thereby (for it were a
most wicked & impiouse thing
so to say) but that through this
meanes especially, we mought
be able to be partakers of that
grace, satisfaction & redemptiõ,
the whiche he by the Sacrifice
of his holie Crosse obteined &
merited for vs, and that therby
it mought be graunted vs, to
haue for a continual meate the
selfe same flesh of his glorified,
whiche for vs suffered death,
with encrease of such graces, &
benedictions, as by it our Lord
shall vouchsafe daily to geue
vs. The second difference is,
that our Lord offered him selfe
visibly on the Crosse, by suffe=
ring and shedding his bloud :
but in the Sacrifice of the Al=
tar,

Differen-
tia se-
cunda.

tar, he offereth him selfe inui=
sibly, and without suffering, by
presenting in himselfe the me=
morie of his Death vnto his
Father. And this is a true Ob=
lation and Sacrifice, although
neither any death be conteined
Rom. 6. in it (bycause Christ can die no
more) neither is any shedding
of bloud in the hoste whiche is
offered, forasmuch as in y Old
Lawe also, many Sacrifices
were done, wherein no bloud
was shed, as in al those Sacri=
fices whiche were made with
wheatē flower or meale, which
were expresse figures of thys
Sacrifice, whereof we do now
entreate : and likewise in that
Sacrifice of one of the twoo
Exod 16. Goates, or one of y two Spa=
rowes, which was let go freely
without death or any shedding
of bloud in the same. In al o=
ther pointes this Oblation of
the Altar is nothing els, but y
selfe

selfe same which Christ offered
on the Crosse , although the
only manner of doing it be di=
uerse and vnlike.

Now if we should saie , that
al this Mysterie , whiche was
instituted in the Supper of our
Lord, required no other thing,
then onely the participation of
his blessed Bodie , or (which is
more horrible to be imagined)
if wee should saic, that wee re=
ceaue it only in a figure : then
nothing els shoulde remaine
therof vnto vs, but only a bare
memory of eating his last Sup
per : & the remembrance of his
Oblation made on the Crosse,
should wholy be cancelled and
strike out of minde. For in this
Sacrifice, the Oblation is one
thing, & the manducatiō or ea=
ting is an other:yea (which is
more)true māducatiō or eating
can not be, vnlesse there be first
made some Oblation , as wee
                              may

may gather by the woordes of
S. Paule speaking of the Old
sacrifices, & of this our New.
1.Cor.10. See (saith he) Israel according
to the flesh. They that eate the
Hostes, are they not partakers
of the Altar? that is to witte,
of the things which are first offered vp and sacrificed?

By taking this therefore to
be done in a figure onely, by-
1.Cor.10. sides that it should be a retur-
ning againe vnto Judaisme,
for that ẏ Jewes did eate their
Manna, and their Sacrifices
of fine flower (which did signifie Christ) onely in a figure and
spiritually: ẏ same also should
not bee a receauing of the true
Sacramente of the Bodie of
Christe, bycause that vnder it
should not be cōteined the very thing of the Sacramēt spoken of & expressed by our Lord,
which is the Bodie of Christe:
whereby shoulde also ensew,
that

that neither any efficacie were
in the woꝛde of God , neither
the annuntiation of his death
ſhoulde directly be made , nei=
ther any offering oꝛ Oblation
ſhoulde bee pꝛeſented to God,
neither finally any other true
meate ſhoulde bee receiued in
this moſte high Sacramente,
moꝛe then is receaued by the
only thinking of Chꝛiſtes Paſ=
ſion, ⁊ by ſimply beleuing in it.

The expoſition of certaine places of S. Paule , whiche
doo appertaine to
this matter.

Cap. XVIII.

IT may ſeeme, that ſome dif=
ficultie oꝛ doubte may here
be moued by the wooꝛdes of
S. Paule wꝛitten vnto the Heb.7.
Hebꝛewes : that, whereas our 9.10.
Loꝛd and Redemer hath once
ben offered vp foꝛ al, ⁊ hath by Obiectio
that one Oblatiō geuen vs foꝛ
F   euer

euer true & perfect satiffaction,
it is no moze necessarp to make
anp new Oblation againe, as
Aaron did, in the bloude of an
other. Yea mozeouer fozaf-
much as he is a Pzieft foz euer
after the ozder of Melchifedech
without a companiõ oz succef-
four: it map seeme, p̃ some honour is derogate & take awap
from the Pzieſthood of Chziſt,
bp conſtituting other Pzieſtes.

Refpon.
Quę res
requirũ-
tur ad in
telligen-
dum ver
bũ Dei.

we therefoze foz a declaration of the truth herein, and a
resolution of this difficultie, do
saie: Firſt, that to vnderſtand
wel and sincerely the wozde of
God, bysides the humilitie,
prayer, and ſtedfaſt faith in the
Catholike Churche (which are
things aboue al other requiſite
to take wozthp frute thereof)
we ought also deepelp to conſider and wep manp circum-
ſtances in the same: as the per-
fon, and intention of the wzi-
ter,

ter, the time in the which it is writen, & the hearers to whom he wrote or sente it. By the intention of the writer, we come to the knowledge of the matter whereof he entreateth. By the helpe of this foundation it shal be easie for vs, so to regulate & frame our minde, that it erre not from the marke & scope of the truth. S. Paule therefore, being an Apostle sente of our Sauiour to establish his Gospel, the foundation and principal ground wherof is, to beleue, that Christ is ẙ true Messias, who was both prophecied of before by the Prophetes, and figured also by diuerse & sundry figures, & that by him only ẙ redemptiõ of the world ought to be made: & wheras this foũdation was first to be laid, before he shuld come to reason of ẙ Sacramẽts & other things of ẙ new Law: vpõ this occasion

F ij　　the

The Apostle writeth to ye Hebrewes at that time, when as they (notwithstanding Messias had suffered and fulfilled euery Olde Sacrifice) did yet continew and vse the Sacrifice of brute beastes in the Temple of Jerusalem, after the Order and Priesthoode of Aaron, whiche was then worne out and expired.

Now to the ende therefore that the Jewes might leaue & abandon those their olde shadowes : S. Paule doth oppose against them with three obiections or Argumentes , endeuouring thereby to perswade & enforme them of the veritie.

The first is , to make them to acknowledge the veritie & truth of the Lawemaker, the which not as a meere man and seruaunt (as Moyses was) but as the true Sonne of God, and true mã, ought to be acknowledged

ledged and taken for the King
of righteouſneſſe and peace.

The other Argument dooth
appertaine to the Lawe, the
which in the Olde Teſtament
(as he ſaith) brought nothing
vnto perfection, and therefore
ought they to receaue an other
Lawe more perfecte, of him
whiche was a more perfecte
Lawmaker.

The thirde is touching the
Prieſthoode, whiche is tranſ-
ferred together with the Law.
So that wheras the Old Law
doth now ceaſe, it is neceſſary,
that the Prieſthood of Aaron
ceaſe alſo. And conſequently,
ſith ẏ New Law taketh place :
it can not be, but that of right
the new Prieſthood ought alſo
not onely to bee accepted of all
men, but to continew, ſo long
as the new Law it ſelfe conti-
nueth : which is, for euer, after
the Order of Melchiſedech.

F v   By

By these forcible and necessary Argumentes (as it were by certaine assured and faithful guides of the truth) & also by the perpetuall Priesthoode of Christ, doth S. Paule declare, that the carnal succession of the Leuiticall Tribe is no more necessarie nor requisit: whereuppon , by the Oblation of Christe made on the Crosse, he concludeth, that an ende is already made of al the Olde and Legal Sacrifices,& that therefore it is an extreme follie and madnesse,to offer vp any more suche kinde of Oblations , to the entent thereby to deserue Gods mercie, and to doo satisfaction for our trespasses, especially syth God our Sauiour hath once geuen and offered vppe him selfe to be a full Sacrifice and Redemption of all mankinde : the whiche one Oblation was the whole treasure

ſure and accompliſhment of all
the ſatiſſactions and remiſſi=
ons of the worlde.

And this only was here the
entention and full purpoſe of
S. Paule, to the ende that the
knowledge of Chriſte beeing
once perſwaded, and the faith
of the true Meſſias, and our
King being throughly plaſed:
he might the more eaſily inſi=
nuate him ſelfe to ſhewe them,
by other Prophecies and Fi=
gures (eſpecially by that of
Melchiſedech) what Oblati=
on or Sacrifice it is, whiche
nowe remayneth vnto Chri=
ſtians: the whiche finally he
ſignifieth in the laſt Chapiter
of that Epiſtle, making men=
tion of the Altar of the Chri=
ſtians, whereof (ſaieth hee)
they can not participate, which
dooe ſerue the Tabernacle,
that is to witte, doo ſerue
the ſacrifices and offeringes
F iiij   of

of beastes, which do nothing at all auaile them that doo serue therein.

Modus obserua- tus ab Aposto- lis in prę- dicando. This selfe same manner of teaching and perswading did the other Apostles vse also in shewing the Incarnation of Chꝛist, and in perswading the other Articles which do apper= taine to the faith of the blessed Trinitie: foꝛcing the hearers firste with suche pꝛeambles as heere S. Paule dooth, befoꝛe they came to the point to teach vs the very meanes lefte vs of our Sauiour, whereby wee might be partakers of the me= rites, which were purchaced ⁊ gotten by him. Neither was there any other occasion but this, that made the Apostles to make so seldome times men= tion of the Pꝛiesthoode of the Chꝛistians, fearing least per= haps vnder this name, mighte be vnderstood that Pꝛiesthood

of

of the Lawe of Moyses, the
which continually (as a thing
vnlawfully kept in vse) they
endeuoured by all meanes to
suppresse and extinguish.

　　whereuppon nowe by the
name of Presbyter, at one time
by the name of Pastor, at an o=
ther by the name of a Bishop,
they vnderstoode that dignitie
of Priesthod, which afterward
S. Dionyse, S. Clement, S.
Ignatius, S. Polycarpe, and
other scholers of the Apostles,
did most plainely expresse, and
after them their Successours,
(then especially, when ẙ Teple
of Ierusalem was destroyed,
and when the vse of the Iewes
Oblations ceased) cōformably
to that, which our Sauiour de=
nounced and foresaied shoulde
come to passe.

　　In this selfe same sorte doth
S. Paule here write in ẙ place
that is obiected : who as in

F v　　　　wri=

ad Tim.
1. Tim. 5.
1. Pet. 2. 3
Act. 14.

writing to the Romaines, and reprouing woorkes, but extolling faith, did not so meane it, that all kinde of workes were vtterly to be neglected: but only condemned those woorkes, which were of ẏ Law of Moyses and of the Gentiles, wherin they, and emong them the Jewes, did pretend only to be iustified without the faith of Jesus Christ: so writing here vnto the Hebrewes, dothe he perswade and commende one Oblation, not to extinguish ẏ vse of the same (which was instituted of our Sauiour & obserued of al true Christiãs) but to abrogate, abolish and take away the Sacrifice of the Old Law. And therfore he writeth after vnto the Romaines, that not the hearers, but the woorkers shalbe iustified: which is to saie, they which doo good workes with a liuely faith: &
vnto

vnto the Hebrewes he decla-   Heb. vi̇.
reth, that we haue a better and
a more excellente Aultar then
they, as I haue said before.

How the place of S. Paule is to
be vnderstood, where he sheweth, that our Sauiour is a
Priest without a
Successour.

Chap. XIX.

OVr Lorde Iesus Christ
is a Priest after y͂ Or-
der of Melchisedech, &
was consecrated of his
Father without a successour &
companion, y͂ is, without any
one, by whose succession, he
should at any time cease to be a
Priest, & without hauing any
person in his companie, which
may be equal vnto him, or haue
the same dignitie or state of
Priesthoode, whiche he hath,
as it was in the Priesthood of
Aaron, whiche successiuely (as
the

the high Priestes died) wente
from one to the other in the
Tribe of Leui: whereas our
Lord hath contrarily a perpe=
tual Priesthood, bycause he re=
maineth and liueth perpetual=
ly , euermore appearing vnto
his Father a continuall inter=
cessour for vs.

The which thing being thus,
we must not vnderstand Christ
to be in such sort a Priest , that
he vseth his Priesthood in his
owne person onely , and in no
mans els. For he vseth the ex=
ercise thereof both in himselfe,
& in his members also. wher=
vppon S. Augustine moste ex=
cellently to this purpose, saith:
De ciuit. Our Sauiour would , that the
Dei.c.20 Sacrifice shoulde be daily fre=
lib.10. quented in his Churche , foras=
much as he himself is y head of
the same bodie, & the selfe same
bodie of the same Head, as wel
that for him , as he for that , in
vie

bie daily to be offred. And tru=
ly what other Priesthod or Or=
der for euer, after the Order of
Melchisedech should be obser=
ued of Christe , if this bee not,
which is the most mystical and
truest Oblation that may be?

Thus also witnessed S. Iohn
Baptist of our Lorde , saying :
This is he , which baptiseth in
the holie Ghoste : and yet did
the Apostles also baptise, vsing
their ministerie and function vi=
sibly therein , by the helpe and
grace of God working in them.
And therefore as the Celestiall
Father sente our Sauiour , so   Ioan.20.
did our Sauiour sende them.
He preached and planted his
Churche in them , and in them
wrought miracles : whiche all
redounded to his owne grea=
ter glorie, and honour , in that
he woulde vouchesafe to com=
municate his power and ver=
tue with so poore and simple
                         men,

men, in whome he loosed & remitted sinnes, and in whom he
offred vp him selfe to God his
Father: & therefore called them
by the name p̄ was due & con-
Matt.5.   uenient to hinself. Ye are (saith
he) the light of the worlde : to
you do I geue p̄ keies of heaue:
to you do I geue my holy spi-
M att.18.   rit : to whom soeuer you remit
sinnes, they shal be remitted.
Ioan. 21.   To S. Peter he said thre times,
Feede my sheep. And you with
Matt.19.   me (saith he) shalbe Iudges in
the last Iudgemēt, to iudge the
twelue Tribes of Israel. And
therfore vnto his Father with
a most vehement & earnest pe-
tition (which was, as S. Paule
saith, heard for p̄ reuerence due
vnto him) maketh his request,
Ioan. 17.   that his Apostles may be one
thing with him, as he is one &
p̄ self same thing with his Father. And to shew p̄ this vnion
which he wrought in vs, ought
to

to continue for euer, he addeth:
Not for theſe onely do I make
requeſt (that is, for y Apoſtles)
but for them alſo, whiche by
their woordes ſhall beleeue in
mee.

This great Prieſt therefore
remaineth a liue for euer, ſith
in vs that be Prieſts, he vouch=
ſafeth (through y infinit great=
neſſe of his mercie) to offer vp
himſelf, who is the only Obla=
tion, that ſhall endure ſo long,
as expiation or ſatisfaction for
ſinne doth endure: that is (as
S. Paule declareth) ſhall en=
dure vntill ſuche time, as our
Lorde ſhal the ſeconde time be
manifeſted vnto al them, which
doo expecte and looke for him
for ſaluation: comming forth,
as it were, out of the veile of
the Celeſtiall Temple, figured
by Sancta Sanctorum, the Ho=
lie of al Holies.

Cer-

Certaine Testimonies of auncient and holie Fathers, which do confirme the things abouesaid.

Cap. XX.

Hom.7.
in cp.ad
Hebr.

SAint Chrysostome saieth: Neither doo wee offer vp nowe one Lambe, and to morow an other, but euery daie the selfe same: & therefore this is but one onely Sacrifice. For els (bycause Christ is offered vp in many places) we shoulde also saie, that there were many Christes, which in no wise can be so : sith assuredly to the contrary it is moste true, that one Christ is in euery place : who being our Bisshoppe, doth offer vp an hoste to cleanse & make vs voide of sinne : and the selfe same hoste do we offer vp also. And within a fewe wordes after, he addeth in what sorte we do this :

for

for a remembrance, saith he, of
that which was done: that is,
of the death and Passion of our
Sauiour: the which thing vn=
lesse we did as wel offer vp, as
also witnesse and denounce, so
oft times as wee chance either
to receaue for our saluation &
sustenáce, either to offer vp this
selfe same bodie of Christe: we
should not only not enioy any
frute thereof, but also incurre
great danimage, in y̅ we shew=
ed our selues as vnmindeful of
y̅ comanndement of our Lord,
and most vngrateful for the be=
nefites receaued of him.

Epist. 23.

S. Augustine likewise wri=
ting to Bonifacius: Our Lord
(saith he) was once offered vp
in him selfe, and yet the same is
neuerthelesse sacrificed for the
people in the Sacrament, not
only during al the Feastes and
Holie daies of Easter, but also
euery daie. So that whosoeuer
were

were demaunded of this point,
& made answer, that our Lorde
is continually offred in Sacri=
fice: he could nothing at all be
accused of any vntruth or falsh=
hed in so saying. And againe in
an other place: There was be=
fore, as ye know (saith he) the
Sacrifice of the Iewes after ẏ
Order of Aaron, in the Obla=
tions of brute beastes, & that in
a mysterie, bycause ẏ Sacrifice
of the Bodie and bloud of our
Lord (which they know wel ẏ
are faithful, and haue redde the
Holie Gospell) was not yet
come: whereas the same now
is spred throughout the whole
worlde. Set ye therfore before
your eyes two kindes of Sa=
crifices: that, which was after
the Order of Aaron: and this,
which is after ẏ Order of Mel=
chisedech. OEcumenius saith, ẏ
the Prophet would neuer haue
said those wordes in æternum,

In Psal. 3.

Heb. 4.

for

for euer, in consideration of that Oblation or Hoste, which hath ben but once offred vp of God: but that he had had respecte to the Priestes whiche are nowe present, by ye meanes of whom, Christ both doth sacrifice, & is sacrificed daily in such forme & manner, as in his last Supper he him selfe instructed them to make this Sacrifice . Theo= InHeb.6 phylact, expounding how we may vnderstand Christ to be a Priest for euer after the Order of Melchisedech, saith: He is so said, bycause ye Oblation (which is offered euery daie, & shall by the meanes of the Priestes of God be offred vp for euer) hath the selfe same Bishop and high Priest, yea also the very selfe same Host, who for vs did san= ctifie, breake, & distribute him= selfe. And therefore addeth S. Lib.4. Ireneus : The Oblation of cap.31. the Churche, which our Lorde offred

offered vppe is reputed of the
whole worlde to be a pure Sacrifice in the sight of God, and
to be accepted of him.

Conclusions which are gathered out of the former
doctrine.

Chap. XXI.

WE may therefore of
thys former Doc-
trine conclude first,
and saie : that S.
Paule reasoneth vnto the Hebrewes , as touching one only
Oblation made visibly vppon
the Crosse , for the destruction
of sinne: and that therfore this
continual Oblation, whiche is
perpetually made in the blessed
Sacrament, doth nothing at al
derogate from that Sacrifice
of the Crosse , no more then it
doth derogate from this , that
our Lord doth continually appeare

peare (as he witnesseth of him selfe) before the presence & face of God almighty for vs, presenting the memorie (as Theophilact saieth) of his gloriouse death & merites vnto his Father. And as it doth nothing derogate from the only Oblation of the Crosse, that our Sauiour beganne from the hower of his blessed Incarnation to be offered vp continually vnto his Father, and consequently was in al his life, yea also from the beginning of the worlde, in a figure of the Olde Law offered vp vnto the same, sith (as S. Iohn saith) the Lambe was killed before the beginning of the worlde : so is not this our Sacrifice of the Altar preiudicial at all or derogatory to that of Christ on the Crosse.

Secondarily wee may also gather of this aforesaied Doctrine, that not onely God is

not

Psal. 29.

Apoc.13.

2.

not depriued & spoyled of his
honour, in ꝑ he doth vouchsafe
for our great honour & dignitie, to vse herein our labour &
ministery, making vs (through
his infinit goodnesse & mercie)
as it were woorkers together
with him, & (as S. Paul saith)
his coadiutors: but also it doth
augment & encrease his blessed
name & honour, and doth exalt
maruelously ꝑ inestimable benefite he did to vs on ꝑ Crosse:
forasmuch as hereby perpetually we declare, of what dependeth al our saluatiõ, which is,
of ꝑ blessed death of Christ, the
which together wͭ his body, we
offer vp in so worthy a memorie.   Finally we may gather
for a third cõclusion out of this
doctrine, that it redoũdeth to a
greater glorie & honour of our
Lord, when we obey his holie
wordes, which said: Do ye this:
then if (vnder a false pretence)
wee woulde searche to disobey

i.Cor.3.

3.

them, folowing our owne opi=
nions & vaine phantasies, and
not the sincere & pure worde of
his Diuine Maiestie. For by
disobeying, ȳ might be wel said
to vs, which S. Ambrose made
answere to Nouatus ȳ Here= De pœ-
tike, who denied ȳ authority of nit.lib.1.
ȳ Christian Priesthood, as tou= cap.2.
ching ȳ absolutiō, & remissiō of
sinnes. No man (saith he) doth
more iniury to ȳ glory of God,
then he, which doth breake the
cōmaundements of Christ. For
whereas he hath said: whose
sinnes ye do remit, they are re=
mitted vnto them: who doth
greater honour to God, he that
dothe obey his commaunde=
mentes, or he which doth resist
and disobey them.

The names, by the whiche the
Greke Church of most anciét
time, and vniuersally, called the
Masse: and withal is proued
the Sacrifice of the Altar.

Cap. 22.

4. Canon
Apost. 28
Concil.
Gang.
14. epist.
Conci. &
canon.
Ignatius
ad Trall.
Ancyran.
Conc. c. 1
& c. 9.
& Gangr
Syn. c. 7.
Nic. c. 14
Euf. li. 6.
c. 43.
can. 3. 7.
& Nicep.
lib. 6. c. 3.
Dialog.
in Iuda.
Diõ. Eccl
Hierarch
Ignat. ad
Smyrn.
In Epist.
contra
Nestor.

THe Greeke Churche did euer with one voice and assent cal by the name of Liturgia, that which we call the Masse : The whiche name of theirs dothe properly signify, the office and function of a Priest, to whom peculiarly it apperteineth to do Sacrifice, and to offer Oblations vnto God for sinnes, as to the Hebrewes S. Paul doth declare. They called it also Osia, which is to saie, Holie and Celestiall things: by the which name we vnderstand that the Polonians call it euen to this daie.

The Masse was also sometimes called Hierurgeió, which is as much in signification as to saie, a holy operation. With the like name vnto this was it called of Neocesariense Councel, and in like manner of the Nicene Councel, where it speaketh

keth of the Oblation of the bo=
die of Chriſt. Of Euſebius and
of ỹ Apoſtles in their Canons
it was called Proſphora agia,
whiche is, a holie Oblation.
And of Iuſtine the Martyr,
Proſpheromene thyſia (in his
interpretation vpon a place of
Malachias the Prophet, which
apperteineth to this matter)
that is, a Sacrifice whiche is
offred vp of vs. Conformable
vnto S. Iuſtine is S. Diony=
ſius the ſcholer of S. Paule, &
Ignatius the Diſciple of S.
Iohn the Euangeliſt. Of the
Epheſine Councell & S. Gre=
gorie Nazianzene it is named
Anæmatos thyſia, which is, an
vnbloudy Sacrifice, to diſtin=
guiſh it from ỹ bloudy Sacri=
fice of ỹ Croſſe, vpon the which
viſibly, & with ſuffering moſte
bitter agonies, was offered vp
a bloudy oblatiō. For although
both the one & the other Obla=
　　　　B　　　　tion,

Nicene
Concil.
can.14.
Euſeb.
li.6.c.43
Ca.3.&7
Niceph.
li.6.c.3.
Dialog.
in Iuda.

Dionyſ.
eccl. hie-
rarch.
Ignat. ad
Smyrn.
In Epiſt.
contra
Neſtor.
& Greg.
de Fune-
ral. Baſil

A Treatife of the

tion, is the very felfe fame: yet
as touching the fo2me and mã-
ner of offering them, they are
fundjie and diuerfe.

Basil. &
Chrysost.
in Litur-
gia.
Epist. ad
Smyrn.
Epist. ad
Hiero.

S. Chryfoftome and S. Ba-
fill, twoo lightes of the Eaft
Church, and Cy2illus Ierofo-
lymitanus in the fift Catechefe
do cal it Phrictodeftaten thyfiá,
that is, a moft d2eadful Sacrifice. Ignatius calling it a Sacrifice, fheweth, that it is not
lawfull to doo this Sacrifice,

Ecclef.
hist. lib. 1
cap. 38.
In nouel.
Duaren.
lib. 7.

without y authoritie of a Bif-
fhop. Sinefiusvfeth this wo2d
to name it Teleten aporreton,
whiche is, a Sacrifice that is
fecrete and full of Myfteries.
By other names is it alfo vni-
uerfally called Holie, and Mystagogica: and of Picepho2us,
a Sacrifice of the tremend and

C. 3. de
Benefic.
2. Tim. 3

viuificall Myfteries: & of Iu-
ftinianus, Profcomide, that is,
an Oblation: and of S. Paul,
Myfterium fidei, a Myfterie of
the

the faith, ſpeaking of the Dea=
cons & Miniſters of the Altar,
vnto whom it apperteined to
diſpenſe this moſt bleſſed Sa=
cramēt, and to exerciſe ſo high
& great an office in a pure con=
ſcience. S. Denyſe (S. Paules   Ecc.hier.
ſcholer) calleth it Teleten tele=
ton, a moſt abſolute Sacrifice
and Sacrament, by the whiche
we becōme fully perfect, and to
bee vnited with God : foras=
muche as Chriſt himſelfe (who
is the founteine and welſpring
of al grace and benediction) is
preſent in ſo high and worthie
a Myſterie : and therefore alſo
is this moſte Bleſſed Sacra=
mente vniuerſally called Eu-
chariſtia.

Whether this name Maſſe was
vſed in the auncient
and Primitiue
Church.

B ij   This

Cap. XXIII.

THis name Missa, which we terme Masse, is foūd to haue ben vsed of S. Ambrose, about a thow-sand and two hundred yeares agone : of the which worde he so serueth himself, as of a name most generally then vsed, and receaued af al men. I (saith S. Ambrose) was in myne office, and had begunne to celebrate Masse, and to pray God in the Oblation therof, that he would vouchsafe, to geue aide & suc-cour. And the blessed Pope S. Leo (vnder whom was gathe-red and confirmed the Coun-cel of Chalcedon) which is one of the first foure General Coū-cels : It must nedes be (saith he) that some parte of ẙ people be depriued of their deuotion, if by obseruing the custome of one onely Masse a daie, none others can offer vp the Sacri-fice,

Epist. 13.

An. 461.

Epist. 88 & 89.& cp.9.ad Dioscor.

fice, but onely they which gather them selues together in
the morning at the breake of
the daie.

Whie this name Missa, that is
to saie, Masse, is so called
of the Hebrewes and
also Latines.

Cap. XXIIII.

Missah emong the He-
brewes signifieth an
Oblation, and is de-
riued of this woorde
Mas, which is in signification
as much to saie, as a tribute or
offering. This name Missa
therefore was first hereof gene
vnto this Sacrifice, bycause it
was in the beginning celebrated in the Hebrew tongue, vntil the time of Adrian the Emperour. And therfore are there
as yet remaining som Hebrew
woordes in the Masse, besides

the margin:
Deut.16.
Num.15.
S.Procl.
Archiep.
Constāt.
de trad.
Diuinæ
Missæ.
6.Synod.
Gener.
c.31.
Epiphan.
heref.79.
Abd. Isi-
dor. Off.
li.1.c.6.
Greg.in
epist.ad
Episcop.
Syrac.
Ambrof.
epist.33.
Chrysost
in hom,
de Eccl.
& myst.

B iij　the

the proper name thereof, as
Alleluia, Osanna, Sabaoth,
Amen.

Now of the Latines it was
after called Missa, bycause in ẏ
end of it, it is denounced vnto
ẏ people, that the Host (which
is Christ) is of the Priest deli-
uered and offered vp vnto the
celestial Father: and that therfore it is nowe graunted vnto
the people to be dimissed, that
is, to depart: the which thing
was in moste auncient time signified vnto the people by the
Greke Deacon in the end of the
Masse, by saying these wordes
Hite hypolisis esti, that is, departe you, for ye are dimissed.

Athanaſ
Epiſt. ad
ſolitarios
Caſſian.
li.3.c.7.8.

Of the Order and Ceremonies
of the Masse, and by whom
it was so ordeined with
suche Ceremo-
nies.

whereas

Cap. XXV.

Hereas wee haue hitherto by Gods grace, entreated of the chief and principal partes of the Maſſe, and as it were of ẏ ſubſtance therof, which is to witte, of ẏ Conſecration, Oblation, & Cõmuniõ oʒ receauing of it: it remaineth now, that we alſo declare the other partes & ceremonies in the ſame appointed by the Apoſtles, & Chriſtes Churche: which al do proceede, & folow ẏ ſubſtantial inſtructiõ of Chriſt. Theſe partes are: ẏ preparatiõ vnto ẏ Sacrifice, the inſtructiõ of ẏ people, ẏ prouiſion of thoſe things which are to be cõſecrated, which S. Denyſe calleth Proteleia, the praying foʒ all men, and finally, the geuing of thankes, which is the concluſion and finall ſumme of the whole Myſterie.

B iiij   S. Paule

S. Paul when he had shewed that the Christians had a Sacrifice, and that they had together with it, the very bodie & blond of Iesus Christ: he addeth after in this sorte, saying:

And when I shall come, I will geue order for the rest: shewing thereby, that the Apostles had the care and charge committed to them, to prouide and duely to ordeine al such things as mought apperteine to that whiche our Sauiour him selfe had instituted & shewed them. Whiche charge as it was in other things geuen, so especially was it as touching the blessed Masse, which is of more weite & importance, then al the rest.

Wherein that the Corinthians mought nothing at al doubt of this their Apostolical authoritie, he wrote after vnto them, saying: Let man take and esteeme vs, as the ministers of Christ,

1. Cor. 11.

1. Cor. 4.

Vide Missam S. Iacobi.

Christ, and dispensators of the
Mysteries of God. And after
declaring, what things they
were, which were recited whē
the people was assembled and
gathered together to this blessed Sacrifice of the Altar, he
saith: Euery one of you hath
the Psalme, he hath the doctrin,
and the Apocalipse, which is, ẏ
reuelation of the Prophecies,
that was redde for the instruction of the people, he hath also
the tongue, and the interpretation.

    These selfe same thinges,
which here S. Paule mentio-
neth, hath ẏ Catholike Church
euer reteined in this blessed
Sacrament: for as touching ẏ
declaration of that which therin is redde and recited: if that
hath not ben continually vsed,
the want thereof cōmeth both
through the encrease of Christendome, and also by meanes

            B v   of

Dion. ec.
Hierar.

Maxim.
Scoliast.

Iustin.
Martyr.
in Apol.
pro Chri-
stianis.
Origen.
hom. 5.
in Num.

of the colde defire that menne now a daies haue to heare euerie daie the worde of God.

In the entrie or the beginning of the Maſſe we haue the Pſalme or ſome parte thereof, to laude and praiſe God. After haue we the Doctrine, and other partes whiche are for the inſtruction of the people, as Leſſons, Collectes, Propheties, Epiſtles, and Goſpelles, whiche therefore ordinarily are openly recited and redde vnto the people, that the ſaying of the Prophet may be verified of them, which ſaith: they haue ordeined his Teſtament vpon his Sacrifices.

Pſal. 49.

The Creede of the Apoſtles foloweth after this, whiche is a Myſterie and explication of our faith : and conſequently, are other thinges as well for the edifying of the people, as alſo ſtirring them vppe vnto
devo⸗

deuotion. whereuppon S. Paule ſpeaking of this My-ſterie, ſaieth: Let all things be 1.Cor.14 done to edification. Finally, the Generall Councelles and Biſhoppes, ſeeing by altera-tion and proceſſe of tyme, the ſundrie wantes and neceſſe-ties of Chriſtian people, haue like good Fathers and vigi-lant Paſtors ouer their flocke, added (as they by experience ſawe was neceſſarie or expe-diente for the glorie of God, and profitable, eyther for the more edifying of the people, or better manifeſtation of the veritie of their faith) ſome one peece, and ſome an other: as of one was added, Gloria in excelſis, of an other Kyrie elei-ſon, whiche is to ſaie, Lorde haue mercie, and of others, o-ther peeces or Ceremonies, as the holie Ghoſt did enduce and leade them to doo.

In

In the time of the Arrians
heresie it was ordeined, that ẙ
Crede of the Nicene Councell
should be said : In the time of
Macedonius his heresie, was
appointed to be said the Crede
of Constantinople for a better
declaration of our faith . For
wheras the Apostles, & Church
(which is the spouse of Christ)
saw, that it was the pleasure
and wil of our Sauiour, that
this Mysterie should remaine
to vs to be done in remēbrance
of his blessed death & Passion:
they did with such diligence &
industrie order it, ẙ we might
haue and enioy a most fruteful
and liuely memorie thereof.

Nowe as concerning the
vestimentes of ẙ Priest (which
wee reade, that S. Iames the
Apostle, and S. John did vse)
we see the Crosse, the Albe, and
many other things, which are
vsed, to this end, that they may
repre

Marginal notes:
Concil. Nice.

Symbol. Athanas.

Matt. 26.
1. Cor. 11.

Epiph. de heres. 25. & 78.

Eus. li. 3. cap. 31. & li. 10. c. 4.

represente to vs a more liuely and present memorie of Christ, whiche in going to sacrifice him selfe on the Crosse, was driue to beare the like apparel & Crosse for his derision. And wheras the Priest maketh ma= ny signes of the Crosse vppon ý Altar, it is (saith S. Austine) to consecrate the blessed Bodie of our Sauiour, to the end that therby we may remember, that al this mysterie of our redem= ption dependeth onely of the benefite of Christ made on the Crosse: and that our prayers & other good woorkes, whiche therein are directed vnto God, are accepted vnto his Diuine Maiestie, through the vertue of the selfe same Crosse.

what shal I saie of the brea= king of the Hoste into three partes? which signifieth vnto vs meruelouse Mysteries of ý Passion of Christe: that it is

applied

Dionys.
de eccl.
Hierar.
Cle. li. 3.
Cyril.
Hieros.
in 5. Ca=
techesi.

August.
tom. 10.
in serm.
de temp.
in Vigil.
Penteco=
ste. serm.
181.

applyed vnto the whole state of the Churche, as well vnto the liue, as to the deade, and as well vnto the Churche here militāt in earth, as that which is triumphant in heauen. The incorporation that we haue in Christe, the remembrance that wee are wasshed and purified with his bloude, the prayer, which also wee make, that the peple may be incorporate with him, is signified by the Hoste that is dipt in the bloude consecrated. The mixture of both water and wine in the Chalice (bysides ẏ the Apostles shewed that Iesus Christ did the same) it doth also record vnto vs and signifie that treasure, whiche issued out of the side of Christ, of both water and bloud: water to wash vs, and bloude to redeeme vs: the one to purge our sinnes, and the other to geue vs a substantiall drinke, wherby

Cyp.ep.3
lib.2.
Hiero.in
quæst.
Hæbra.
Aug.de
eccl.dog
mat.c.75
Damasc.
lib.4.de
fide or
tho.c.14.

wherby we might be susteined
in this life.

    Thus in conclusion , all
things conteined in this bles=
sed Sacrifice of the Masse , are
full of high Mysteries , whe=
ther they be gestures of reuerence , or eleuation of the eies,
whiche doo put vs in minde of
whom we ought to depend, or
lightes vpon the Altar, where=
by we are aduertised , that our
hartes ought continually to be
bright in puritie , and burning
with the fier of charitie , and
full of the holie Ghoste , which
appeared vnto the Apostles in
tongues of fier.

Theo. in
Ioã.c.14.

Concil.
Carthag.
cap.24.

Fower sortes of praiers are ordeined in the Masse, of S.
Paule, as S. Augustine
and other holie
Writers do
declare.

                S. Paule

Cap. XXVI.

a.Tim.2.

Saint Paul writing to Timothie, exhorteth that aboue all things, obsecrations, orations, postulations, & geuing of thankes be made for al men, for Kings, & for suche as bee in authoritie. The same writing to Timothee then Bishoppe (and left in Grece to order and place the Priests in the Churches there) willeth, that in their prayers, they should vse this forme and manner, which both before had euer ben vsed, and is now also côtinually practised of ŷ church in this high Mysterie of the Masse. Obsecrations (saith S. Augustine) are vsed in the celebration of this blessed Sacrament of the Aultar: Orations are made in time of the Consecration of it: Postulations be when the people is blessed by the Priest: & geuing of thanks

Epist.59.
ad Paulinum.

is,

is, when God is praised and
thanked after celebration, for so
high a Mysterie. And thus is
this place of S. Paule interpreted of the Masse, as well by
S. Chrysostome, which liued a
thousande and two hundred
yeares past, as also by S. Augustine (as ye here see) and S.
Ambrose, and Theophilacte,
Ecumenius, Anselmus, and
others.

That the Apostles said Masse,
and their Successours, from
time to time conti-
nually.

Cap. XXVII.

S Aint Paul saith: We haue Heb. 13.
an Altar, of the which it is
not lauful for them to eate
which do serue the Taber-
nacle: that is, which do serue
any other Sacrifice, then that
which only is of ψ Christians.
And truly, most manifest it is,
that

that the Altar should be super-
fluouse and to no purpose, vnlesse we had somewhat to offer
vp and do sacrifice (as I haue
said before) vppon it. In the
Actes of the Apostles ʒ Grcke
texte hath, that whiles the A-
postles did sacrifice vnto God,
that is, whiles they did celebrate their Liturgie : the holie
Ghoste saide vnto them : Set
yee aparte Paule and Barna-
bie for mee, to doo the functi-
ons, whereunto I haue chosen them.

S. Luke him selfe, whiche
wrote the Actes of the Apostles, teacheth vs, what hee
meaneth by Liturgia, when in
his Gospel he sheweth ʒ office
of Zacharie, the which properly
was to sacrifice. S. Peter said
Masse in Antioche in the Hebrew tongue, which was in effect the very same Masse, which
now we celebrate, except certaine

Textus
commu-
nis habet
ministrāt
tibus illis
Textus
Erasmi
habet:sa-
crifican-
tibus.
Luc.1.
Abdias &
Isido.off.
li.1.c.16.
Greg. in
Epist. ad
Episcop.
Syracu-
sanum &
Remig.
Symeon
quidam
scriptor
Gręcus.

tain additiõs of praiers, which
(as I ſaied before) were wel
added vnto it: for that Maſſe
of S. Peter, was (not without
good cauſe) ſhorter thẽ others,
through the perill of perſecution, which in thoſe daies was
very frequent and common.
Ignatius ſheweth, that Clement and Anacletus ſerued as
Deacons vnto S. Peter, and
Timotheus and Linus vnto
S. Paule, and Stephen vnto
S. James.

The cõmemoration of Mar-
tyrs (as of ẙ mẽbers of Chriſt,
for whoſe faith they dyed) was
after added in the Canon of ẙ
Maſſe, by their Succeſſours.
Nowe, as the mentiõ of the
death of Moyſes made in the
fiue bokes of Moyſes, proueth
nothing to the contrary, but
that thoſe bookes were writen
of him: ſo a cõmemoration in
the Maſſe of S. Peter, as touching

Ad Hie-
ronẽ, &
ad Trall.

S. Procl.
Archiep.
Conſtãt.
de tradit.
diuinæ
Miſſæ.
6. Synod.
gen. c. 32

ching the death of him which
wrote it, denieth not but that
he, of whome the memorie is
made, may be also the Author
of the same.

S. James saied Masse in
Jerusalem, the which forme of
Masse is yet presently extant:
and is longer then all others,
conformably vnto the deuotiō
of that Primitiue Churche,
which did continue in prayer,
as S. Luke saith. S. Andrew
did celebrate the holie Sacrifice of Masse in Achaia: and
therefore made he answere in
this sorte vnto Egeas, which
would make him do Sacrifice
vnto the Idolles and Diuels:
I (saith he) doo sacrifice euery
daie vnto the liuing God euen
that immaculate Lambe, which
was slaine vppon the Altar of
the Crosse, the flesh and bloud
whereof after that the whole
faithful people haue eaten and
drunke:

Epiph.
heref.79.
Ignat. ad
Hieron.
& Tral.
Abd. in
vita An-
dreæ. &
ep.7.dia-
conorū.

dꝛunke : yet doth the Lambe,
which was ſacrificed, remaine
neuertheleſſe whole, and aliue.

Likewiſe did S. Matthew
celebꝛate Maſſe in Aethiopia.
And the Apoſtles Philippe &
Bartholomew (as Nicepho‑
rus wꝛiteth) in Syꝛia, who al‑
ſo did oꝛdeine Biſhops, & geue
Oꝛders vnto Pꝛieſtes in Aſia.
S. John ſaid it in Epheſus, &
made Biſhops and Pꝛieſtes in
diuerſe places. S. Thomas in
India , S. Philippe in Phꝛy‑
gia, S. Bartholomew in In‑
dia, S. Symon in Jeruſalem.
And to be ſhoꝛte, all the other
Apoſtles , where ſo euer they
were, did celebꝛate the Maſſe,
as thereof moſt plaine & mani‑
feſt arguments remaine in the
Hiſtoꝛies to this Daie.

It is a thouſand and foure
hundꝛed yeares, ſithens ẏ holy
Maſſe was ſpꝛead thꝛoughout
the whole woꝛld, as S. Irenee
mak“eth

Marginal notes:

Achaia
& Ano‑
nymus
Philale‑
tus.
Niceph.
li. 2. c. 49
Euſeb.
c. 23. li. 3.
Niceph.
c. 42. li. 2
hiſtor.

Ireneus.
li. 4. c. 32

maketh mention, which liued in the same time. Of S. Marke wee haue a Masse in writing. S. Clement the Martyr and Successour of S. Peter saied, that it was not lawfull to sacrifice in any other place, then where the Diocesan and Bisshop himself should cōmaund. S. Denyse the scholer of S. Paule sheweth, that his Predecessours saied the selfe same Masse in substāce, which now we haue. Of S. Ignatius are moste manifest Testimonies, which wee haue rehearsed before, as are those of Ireneus, and S. Cyprian. Anacletus, which liued in the time of S. Peter, not onely maketh mention of the Priest, and Sacrifice, but also of the holie vestimentes which are vsed in this most blessed Mysterie.

Telesphorus Bishoppe and Martyr, which liued within a hun=

Epist. 3.
de offic.
Sacerd.
& Marc.
Ephesin.
scriptor
antiquis-
simus idē
refert.
Hier. ec-
cles. 3. &
vltimo.

Epist. ad
omnes
Oriētales

hundꝛed and foure and thirtie
yeares after Chꝛiſte, gaue firſte
the oꝛder and foꝛme, which yet
is obſerued, to ſaie thꝛee Maſ=
ſes on Chꝛiſtemaſſe daie : the   Matth. 4
one at midde nighte, to geue
thankes vnto God foꝛ the Na=
tiuitie of our Loꝛde : the other
at the bꝛeake of the daie, foꝛ the
honour which the ſheepherdes
gaue vnto Chꝛiſt by the aduer=
tiſment of the Angels : and the
third in the bꝛoad daie, to ſig=
nifie that the daie of redemptiõ
did appere with ẏ bꝛight ſonne
of rightcouſnes:the which thꝛe
Maſſes doo alſo ſignifie vnto
vs, ẏ the Natiuitie of our Sa=
uiour Chꝛiſt was a perfect ſal=
uatiõ vnto al them, which wer
faithful in ẏ Law of Nature, in
the Lawe of Moyſes, & in the
Law of the Goſpell: foꝛ Ieſus
Chꝛiſt (as S. Paul ſaith) was   Heb. 13.
yeſterdaie, and is to daie, and
ſhal be foꝛ euer.

                      Ter=

Ad Scapulam &
De cultu
fœmi-
narum.

Tertullian, who was in the
yeare of our Lord a hundred &
three score: we (saith he) doo
offer vppe Sacrifice vnto our
God, for the saluation & good
estate of the Emperour. For
the better vnderstāding of the
which woordes, he sheweth in
an other place, that only prayers are not there meant by the
name of Sacrifice, bicause, saith
he, it is not lawful for wemen
to do that Sacrifice, neither to
offer any such Oblation, which
they might well doo, if it were
only to be taken for prayers.

Epist.1.
ad oēs
ortho-
doxos.

Alexander the first, who was
Bishop & Martyr a thousand
foure hūdred and fortie yeares
sithens, and Marcellinus the
Bishop, which was three hundred and seauen yeares after
Christ, doo manifestly in writing declare and set foorth the
vtilitie & frute, that cōmeth by
ẏ blessed Sacrifice of ẏ Masse.
S. Sixtus

S. Sixtus Martyr & Biſhop, did celebrate Maſſe in Rome, & after it, went vnto his Martyrdome. S. Lawrence ſeeing him goe to die, cried out (as S. Ambroſe writeth) with a lowde voice, and ſaid: O Father, whither goeſt thou without thy ſonne? O bleſſed Prieſt whither makeſt thou ſuch haſte to goe without thy Deacon? Thou waſt not wont to do Sacrifice without a Deacon.

Finally, al the holie Fathers & Generall Councels do make like mentiō of this Prieſthood, and Sacrifice, & of the ordinances and ceremonies apperteining vnto the conſecration of the ſame: ſo that to ſtand now in denial of it, is an expreſſe token and ſigne of vtter depriuation of all lighte, knowledge, grace, iudgemente, and faith. S. Baſil, S. Chryſoſtome, and S. Gregorie Nazianzen mai-

Ambr. 1. offic. c. 4

In liturgia & in 16. ho. 77 in Matt. 7

Hom. 26 1. Cor. hom. 2. cap. 2. ad 1. Tim. 1.

H   ſter

AdEphe.
hom.3.
Ad Heb.
hom.79.
& alibi.
li.5.ep 33
ster vnto S. Ierome, and S.
Ambrose maister vnto S. Augustine, wrote their Masses,
which were vsed in Grece, and
in Asia, & now presently are in
Milan: wherein they al praied
for the dead, and made inuocations vnto the Saintes to be
intercessours for them by the
meanes of the blessed merites
of our Sauiour Iesus Christ.

li.5.ep.33
S. Ambrose said: God graunt
of his infinite goodnes, that the
Angell doo presently assist vs
whiles we offer vp the Sacrifice
on the Altar, yea rather that he
shew himselfe visibly vnto vs:
for thou oughtest not to doubt
but that the Angel doth ther assist, wher Christ himselfe is present and offered vp in Sacrifice.

In Luc.1
Tom.6.
cap.28.
lib.20.
contra
Faust.
Maniche
De trinit
li.4.c.13.
S. Augustine, bysides the
places wee haue already alleaged, hath also this: Wherfore
the Christiás (saith he) do celebrate

brate a memory of the ſelf ſame Sacrifice made (**for he ſpake of that of the Croſſe before**) with the Oblation and participation of the body and blud of Chriſt. **And againe in an other place.** What thing (**ſaith he**) is ſo con- uenient to be receaued of men, as humaine fleſh, which offred vp it ſelfe for them? And what thing is ſo apt to this Sacrifice, as mortal fleſh? and what thing is ſo pure and cleane to purge the ſaultes and vncleanneſſe of mortal men, as is the fleſh that was borne in the wombe, and of the wōbe of the bleſſed Vir- gin, without al cōtagion of car- nal concupiſcence? And what thing finally can be ſo grateful- ly offered vp, and taken, as the fleſh of our Sacrifice, made the bodie of our Prieſt? **I omitte here to rehearſe Cyril, Ierom, Hilarie, Euſebius, Gregorie,**

Lib. 4. c. 13. De Trinitat.

D ij   and

and to cóclude, the whole vniuersal Antiquitie of y Church,
the which (as partely I haue
touched aboue) doth with one
mouth and assent declare, this
to be a moste euident and constant veritie.

That the liue are holpen by the Masse.

Cap. XXVIII.

For the proufe hereof, saith
S. Paule: Euery Bishop
that is taken from emong
mé, is cóstituted in things
which do aperteine vnto God,
to the ende he may offer vppe
giftes & Sacrifices for sinnes.
And S. Martialis, which was
one of the Seuentie & two Disciples of Christ, saith : we do
offer vp the Bodie & bloude of
Christe , in lyfe euerlastinge,
whom y Iewes (through ma-
lice & enuie) did sacrifice, thinking thereby to extinguish his
name

Heb.5.

Epist.ad
Burde-
gal.c.3.

name out of the worlde . And
this do we (saith he) set foorth,
sanctified on the holy Altar, for
y̆ cause of our saluatiō: knowing, that by this only remedie,
he will geue vs life.

S. Cyprian saith, that by this
Sacrifice , & by the hand of the
Priest, to whom we make our
confession, both our cōsciences
are purged , & also we brought
to peace and vnitie with God.
S. Augustine proueth y̆ worde
of God to be moste true: that
is , that we are fedde with the
flesh of our Lorde, for life euerlasting : & thereupon he saith :
what shall I saie of the verie
Bodie and bloud of our Lord,
which is an only Sacrifice for
our saluation. S. James, and
S. Ignatius doo in like manner confirme the same.

Cyprian.
Ser. 5. de
lapsis.

Li. 1. c. 15.
contra
Crescon.
lib. 20.
cap. 25.
De ciuit.
Dei. &
li. 4. c. 14
de trinit.
In Missa.
epist. 7.

That the Masse doth helpe
against euil spirites.
D iÿ   Espe-

Cap. XXIX.

Li.22.de
ciuit.Dei
cap.8.

ESperius (saith S. Augustine) a man of the degree of a Tribune, had in the territorie of Fussales, a peece of lande or Lordship, called Cubedi, in the which being aduertised, that his house and familie, which there remained, was much molested with euill and maligne spirites, whiche gaue great affliction, and dammage, as wel vnto his beasts & cattel, as also vnto his seruãts whome hee there entertcined: requested, saith S. Augustine, our Priests in my absence, that som one of them would vouchsafe to goe thither, to whose praiers those euil and maligne spirites might yelde and be expelled from thence. whervpon (saith he) one wente, and there offered vp the Sacrifice of the blessed bodie of Christ, praying him with al intercession and in

most

moſt feruẽt wiſe that he could,
to finiſh that trouble : ẏ which
by and by (through the mercie
of God) did ceaſſe.

That the Maſſe doth helpe mer-
uelouſly the ſowles of the
dead which are in
Purgatorie.

Cap. XXX.

That this is true, it is
firſt proued by the con=
tinuall Catholike faith,
and generall practiſe of
ẏ Church, which hath alwaies
endured euen from the time of
the Apoſtles, ẽ their Diſciples,
who did cuſtomablie pray in
their Maſſes for ẏ dead. This
much doth ſ. Dioniſe, who was
the Diſciple of S. Paule, ſhew.
Likewiſe Tertullian, whiche
was an hundred yeares before
S. Cypriã, ẽ a ſcholer alſo of ẏ
Apoſtles, ſaith : we make Ob=
latiõs for the dead in their An=
niuerſa-

Eccl. Hi-
erar. c.7.
Papias
diſci. Ioã.
Euangel.
li. de co-
rona mi-
litis. vxor
& de mõ
nogamia
& de ex-
hortat.
ad caſti.

D iiij

A Treatise of the

In liturg
li.1.ep.9.
& de du-
pli. Mar.
li.3.c.75
Li.quæst
34.qu.

niuersaries. Basil in like sorte, and others, do in their Masses make manifest mention of the same: as namely S. Cyprian, & Epiphanius, which was in the yeare of our Lord three hundreth and ninetie. And Athanasius, who was one of the chiefest Prelates in the Nicene Councel.

Hom.3.
ad Phili.
& idem
in ho.69.
ad pop.
Antioch.
& ho.41.
1.ad Cor.
& ho.21.
in Act.
Apost.

It is most worthie of note, that S. Chrysostome writeth of this same matter: It was not for naughte (saith he) establisshed of the Apostles, that in the celebratiõ of the venerable and tremende Mysteries a memorie should be made of them, which are departed out of this life. For they well knew, that it would be very profitable, and muche auailable vnto them. Of S. Ambrose wee haue so plaine & euident Testimonies, as well in his Masse, as also where he speaketh of y̆ death of the

the Emperours Gratian and
Valentinian, and in his prayer
vpon the death of Satirus, and
els where in his workes, that
no man can doubt thereof.

But aboue al others, S. Augustine doth moste manifestly
proue this, who besides that he
had with Epiphanius declared
Aerius for an Heretike, in that
he denied praiers and oblatiōs Li.5.ep.
to be auailable, which ÿ Chri- cap.17.
stian Church made for ÿ dead, De heref.
he also saith these woordes: It ad Quod
must not be denied (saicth hee) uultdeū.
but that the sowles of the de- Enchir.
parted are holpen by the chari- c.10. &
tie and deuotiō of them which serm.10.
are aliue, when they offer vppe De verb.
the Sacrifice of our Mediatour Apoſt.&
Iesus Christe for them. The lib. de
same also in his Bokes of Con cura pro
fessions not only sheweth, that mortuis.
Monica his Mother requested cap.1.
at her death, that the Sacrifice Lib.9.
of the Masse shuld be offred vp Confeſſ.
                                cap.11.12
     P v   for   13. & vlt.

for her soule, but also praieth the Readers (meaning Priests) that they woulde vouchsafe to accōplish that his mothers desire: & emong other things addeth furthermore these words, speaking of his mother Monica: Shee (saith hee) desired, that a memorie should be made of her at the Altar, where shee knew, that that Holie Oblation was dispensed and offred vp, by the which the sentence that was geuen againste vs, is cancelled and striken out. And this selfe same thing he sheweth a while after more plainly, saying: that the Sacrifices of the Altar, and good workes are propitiatorie for the soules of them whiche were not very euil in their life: that is, which are not condemned to hel.

To holie Paulinus he affirmeth the same, and also addeth for

Ad Paulinū. li 18 cap.36. De ciuit. Dei.& li.20.c.9 & ep.64.

for a corroboration thereof, the word of God in ẏ Machabees, which a'though the Iewes do not accept, yet (as S. Ierome & S. Auguſtine ſaie) the Chriſtiaus do accepte, who do take no directió of their faith of the Infidelies, but of the true and Catholike Church of God, which alwaies is directed and gouerned of the holie Ghoſt.

2.Mach. cap.12. Hierō.in Prol. in Machab. Aug.de ciuit.Dei

FINIS.

RESPICITE VOLATILIA COELI, ET PVLLOS CORVORVM